ESSEX
WITCHES

PETER C. BROWN

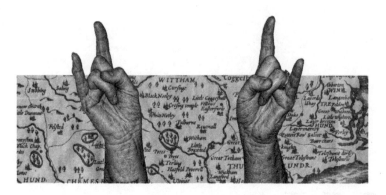

© Jasmine Hurst, Julie Chirila, Bernard Browne

First published 2014

The History Press
The Mill, Brimscombe Port
Stroud, Gloucestershire, GL5 2QG
www.thehistorypress.co.uk

British Library Cataloguing in Publication Data.
A catalogue record for this book is available from the British Library.

ISBN 978 0 7524 9980 2

Typesetting and origination by The History Press
Printed and bound by TJ International Ltd, Padstow, Cornwall

Contents

Introduction

Medieval folk had long believed that the Devil was carrying out his evil work on earth with the help of his minions, and in 1484 Pope Innocent VIII declared this to be the truth in his papal bull *Summis Desiderantes*, which promoted the tracking down, torturing and executing of Satan worshippers. However, it was perhaps the reign of the son of Mary, Queen of Scots, James VI of Scotland and I of England that could be described as the 'age of witchcraft' in Great Britain. During the Tudor and Stuart period, Essex was an extremely religious county, and everyone – including the great, the wise and the learned – believed in witches. James VI of Scotland was a staunch Protestant who had narrowly escaped death in the winter of 1589 during strong winds and huge waves that severely buffeted his ship while on the North Sea. He believed, having been exposed to witch-hunting while in Denmark, that he was the target of a satanic conspiracy by sorcerers and witches who used black magic because of the way the ship behaved in the storm.

Upon his return to Scotland, James put into effect the practices carried out in Denmark and most of the Continent, namely the witch trials, and so began the wholesale persecution of witches.

As his paranoia about the Devil's plot to kill him grew, James personally interrogated witches from the town of Trenton, including Geillis Duncane, Agnes Sampson of Paddington, Agnes Tompson of Edinburgh, James Fian (alias John Cunningham), Barbara Napier and Effie MacClayan, all of whom he believed to be Satan's students. On his orders they were tortured to confess their part in plotting his demise. Following this he wrote a three-part working of his studies titled *Daemonologie*, which was published in 1597 and became something of a handbook for witch-hunters for identifying and destroying witches.

In 1604 he repealed the statute introduced by Elizabeth I, under which hanging was the punishment for those convicted of causing death by witchcraft, and replaced it with a more severe charter, that simply the practice of witchcraft was enough to cause a person to be hanged. Between 1603 and 1625 there were about twenty witchcraft trials a year in Scotland – nearly 450 in total. Half of the accused were found guilty and executed.

The legacy of James's *Daemonologie* continued throughout the seventeenth century and led to the torture and execution of hundreds of women in a series of infamous witch trials. No one knows exactly how many died during this period, such as at the Pendle trial of 1612, or how many others were killed in cases that never came to court.

The fear of witches as the allies of Satan and his demons grew because of the hatred between the rival factions within the Church, when the Protestants and Catholics were literally at each other's throats. The urge to eliminate evil spread very rapidly across Western Europe, and in France and Germany tens of thousands were sentenced to a terrible death. Witch-hunting was also widespread across Scotland and England, but most notably in Essex, which became the hub of witchcraft activity. Between 1560 and 1680 there were over 700 people involved in cases of witchcraft in Essex, either as a suspect or a victim, and of these over 500 were prosecuted at the assizes, quarter sessions, or ecclesiastical courts. In 1645 alone, there were thirty-six witch trials in Essex.

Political and religious chaos reigned throughout the period of the English civil wars (1642–51) and it was against this background of religious upheaval, caused in part by the Protestant Reformation and the Catholic Counter-Reformation, that the previously unheard-of Mathew Hopkins of Manningtree assumed the title of Witch-finder General in 1645. Witch-hunting throughout England was a judicial operation, but occasionally agitated villagers would take justice into their own hands, executing suspected witches in a vigilante style. However, after Hopkins took on the witch hunts, this rarely happened. His reputation spread far and wide and he had a profound impact on those around him. No one was safe from an accusation of witchcraft and marginalised women bore the brunt of it. Hopkins made a very lucrative living from it.

Note on the text: I have used the term 'English civil wars' in the plural in this book because although it is recognised as one war, between 1642 and 1651 there were, in fact, three separate wars. The 1642–46 and 1648–49 wars pitted the supporters of King Charles I against the supporters of the Long Parliament, and the conflict of 1649–51 saw fighting between supporters of King Charles II and those of the Rump Parliament.

ONE

ENGLAND
AFTER THE TUDORS

The Stuart period of British history refers to the period 1603–1714 in England (in Scotland it began in 1371). Elizabeth I, the last of the Tudor monarchs, died on 24 March 1603. Having never married, she had no descendants and so her two kingdoms of England and Ireland were left to be ruled by her closest heir, the Scottish king James VI.

James's greatest fear in life was a violent death. His childhood and adolescence were unhappy, abnormal and precarious; he had various guardians, whose treatment of him differed widely. Though his education was thorough, it was heavily weighted with strong Presbyterian and Calvinist political doctrine, and although he was highly intelligent and sensitive, he was also shallow and vain. In 1582, he had been kidnapped by Scottish nobles and only escaped the following year. This kept James's fear for his life at the forefront of his mind.

A suitable queen was found for James in Anne of Denmark, and they were married by proxy in July in 1589. Arrangements were then made for the new princess to come to England, but as she set out, she was detained on the coast of Norway by a violent storm. James sailed to Upsala, and, after a winter in the north of the Continent, brought his bride to Scotland in the spring of 1590, but not without encountering more rough weather.

There were rumours that plots had been made against James over his alliance, and witches were accused of attempting to drown him by calling up a storm while he was at sea with his new wife. Several people, most notably Agnes Sampson, were convicted of using witchcraft to send storms against James's ship. James became obsessed with the threat posed by witches and,

King James I of England and VI of Scotland, by John De Critz the Elder.

inspired by his personal involvement, in 1597 he wrote the *Daemonologie*, a tract that opposed the practice of witchcraft.

The infamous Gunpowder Plot to blow up the House of Lords during the State Opening of England's Parliament on 5 November 1605 further endorsed his fear and paranoia, and he signed an order that the captured conspirators should endure the minor tortures first and that the torturers should then move on to the more extreme measures to extract a confession. The public execution of those conspirators who were caught was a stern reminder of what would happen to anyone else foolish enough to involve themselves with treason.

The Stuart period was the beginning of a dramatic gap between the rich and the poor in England. At the top of society were members of the nobility, who owned huge amounts of land and commanded a lot of political power and influence because the government could not keep up with the rising costs of the civil wars, so had turned to them for support. The rents from royal lands could only be raised when the lease ended, which placed MPs in the position of refusing to raise money unless the king bowed to their demands.

The situation was further complicated by religion. The English Puritans were pleased when James I took the throne, for he had been brought up in Scotland by strict Protestants, men like themselves. They hoped that he would 'purify' the Church of England of its remaining Catholic elements, but no changes were made. Although he was a Protestant, James disagreed with many of their views, believing in the divine right of kings, and that God had chosen him to rule. Although he was willing to work with Parliament, he believed that ultimate authority rested with him.

DÆMONOLOGIE,
IN FORME
OF A DIA-
LOGVE,
Diuided into three books:

WRITTEN BY THE HIGH
and mightie Prince, IAMES by the
grace of God King of England,
Scotland, France *and* Ireland,
Defender of the Faith, &c.

LONDON,
Printed by *Arnold Hatfield* for
Robert VVald-graue.
1 6 0 3

Written by King James I and published in 1597, the original edition of *Daemonologie* is widely regarded as one of the most interesting and controversial religious writings in history.

THE ENGLISH HIERARCHY SYSTEM

Below the nobles of society were the lords of the manor (or gentry) and the rich merchants, who became steadily richer as trade and commerce became an increasingly important part of the English economy. These gentlemen owned large amounts of land and they were usually educated and had a family coat of arms. The monarchy relied on them to keep law and order, and they would sit as judges in the local courts. They would also control food prices and collect the taxes that were used to help the poor, although it was beneath their dignity to do any manual work. In the sixteenth century there was no National Health Service and no old age pension. Nor was there unemployment or child benefit. Instead, each town had alms-houses and hospitals to look after the old and sick. Rich merchants often left money to almshouses in their wills.

Below the gentry were yeomen and craftsmen. Yeomen were the better-off villagers who owned their own pieces of land. Often able to read and write, they could also be as wealthy as gentlemen. They would pay labourers to work their farms, but would also work alongside them.

Then there were the tenant farmers, who owned no land of their own, but would lease strips of land from the rich to grow their own produce while earning a wage working for the lords or the yeomen. They were often illiter-ate and very poor, and life for them was very hard, with around 50 per cent of them living at subsistence level – having just enough food, clothes and shelter to survive.

Labourers were at the bottom end of the scale. They worked full time for landowners for very meagre wages and could afford to eat meat perhaps three or four times a week, the very poor perhaps only once a week. For at least part of the time they had to live on poor relief, which came after assessment by overseers or parish officers. In the villages, their homes were simple shacks made of clay, with wooden walls and a thatched roof. They could keep a cow or sheep on the common land, and their income would be supplemented by their wives, who would spin wool or churn butter as a way to pay rent and buy bread.

Farming in medieval England was very crude and hard, but it was critically important to a peasant family. The farmers had to carry out specific tasks throughout the year to ensure the best possible yield from the land they worked, which was invariably owned by the lord of the manor. There was plenty of land around the villages and the farmers grew crops needed to supply the towns in exchange for money they had to pay in rent of the land and taxes to the church, called a tithe, which was approximately ten per cent of what they earned. It was the tithe tax that was very unpopular, and it meant the difference between living and just about surviving after their dues were paid. What was left over could be kept, although the seeds for the following year's crop had to be purchased.

Sheep, cattle, oxen and pigs were kept on many holdings, and these animals were invaluable to the farmer. In fact, they were more important to them and their day-to-day existence than their children; the loss of one animal would have been catastrophic. The animals were kept indoors at night because, if left outside, they would have just wandered off or been stolen. This made for a very unhygienic environment as there was no running water, toilets or a bath, but despite disease being common, it kept the animals safe.

The towns of the Stuart period were dirty, unsanitary and crowded, with the constant odour of rotting vegetables and effluent from the horses that drew carriages and carts. Water was usually obtained from wells, and some towns had conduits that brought in water from the countryside for the public to use. Houses were packed together in narrow lanes, and people were packed into the houses; ten to a room was not uncommon. There were no sewers and no drains, and offal and dirty water were thrown into the streets, providing perfect breeding places for black rats. The fleas that lived on the rats carried bubonic plague, which would quickly kill the people it infected. At night, carts would make their way through the streets and you would hear the mournful cry, 'Bring out your dead.' The plague was not over until 1665, when it was found that brown rats, whose host pests did not carry the disease, could drive the black rats from the towns.

The implementation of the Poor Law, which was the system for the provision of social security in operation in England and Wales from the sixteenth century, specifically defined the 'poor' and categorised them into three groups. These were 'the impotent poor', who could not work and provide for themselves, 'the able-bodied poor', those who were capable of labour but who could not find work, and 'the vagrants' – the beggars.

The Poor Law made provisions to offer relief and to provide materials to these people, of whom there were a significant number, and the resulting social improvements would have been a contributing factor in the decline of witch hunts as England, and indeed much of Europe, made the transition from early modern to modern times.

AGRICULTURE, FARMING LIFE AND WORK

Almost all farmers kept pigs, and most also owned a few cows and goats for milk and cheese, and sheep for their wool, grazing the animals on common land if permission was granted by the lord of the manor. Chickens were also kept for their eggs, and when the livestock came to the end of its effective productive life – when the number of eggs declined and the quality of the milk or wool became poor – it was slaughtered, salted and stored. This was usually done in the autumn because during the winter months the family and the animals had to try to survive on whatever food could be saved through a non-growing season.

The farmers also grew crops on arable land for their own food, and a small amount extra to take and trade in the town markets. This enabled them to buy from craftsmen what they could not make themselves, such as boots, hats, pots and pans, and harnesses for the livestock they used to plough the land. Daily life on the farm was a hard grind, and routines were dictated by the weather and the seasons, influencing the amount of daylight available for farming work. A field rotation system was used for growing wheat, oats and rye for cereals and breads, and, when mixed with vegetables, a dish called 'pottage' – a staple diet of the poor. Barley was grown for making beer. The water in this time period was so unsafe that beer was a very common beverage drunk by nearly all – children included. Life expectancy during this period was forty years.

By springtime, most people were on restricted rations of a very monotonous diet. Early garden vegetables were considered a great treat, but a bad storm or lack of rain at the wrong time could seriously reduce the crops available. The vegetables that would have been grown included carrots, parsnips, onions, and beetroot (turnips were not widely used until around the 1750s).It was here that the farmer, his wife and older children had to be multi-skilled, and they relied heavily on sharing the work with neighbours and hired labour, especially at harvest and market time. Foods, both vegetable and animal, were available only at certain times of the year.

Potatoes had become available, but were not trusted by the farmers; this 'new' vegetable was considered to be downright evil and was believed to cause leprosy, narcosis and early death. It took nearly 200 years before it was widely accepted as a beneficial vegetable. Even in Europe potatoes were regarded with suspicion, distaste and fear. Generally considered to be unfit for human consumption, they were used only as animal fodder and sustenance for the starving. Tomatoes, too, were treated with suspicion by farmers. Despite having been introduced to England around the 1590s, they took a long time to be accepted into rural farming communities as they were believed to be poisonous (they belong to the nightshade family of plants).

The wife's lot was no less than the farmer's. She would bake bread, make pickles and conserves from preserve vegetables, brew beer, and if they were as wealthy as yeomen, keep bees for honey.

Beliefs and Modern Science

The class system was thought by all people to have been formed by God and that he had given it his blessing. Parents also believed that the word of the Bible provided instructions for taking care of their children. Another widely held opinion was that if you were unmarried, you were living in sin, which is why girls were married off at a very young age. However, fear of the unknown, moral panic, and belief in magic created many superstitions, many of which are still used today. For example, saying, 'God bless you' after someone sneezed derived from people's belief that the Devil could enter your body when you sneezed, and that those words warded it off. A black cat crossing your path is thought to be unlucky because of the belief of their association with witches. Walking under a ladder is also considered unlucky; in the sixteenth century it reminded people of the gallows and executions. Breaking a mirror would bring bad luck for seven years because mirrors were considered to be tools of the Gods. Subsequently, ideas of witchcraft as heresy found a very receptive audience who believed that certain people, such as shamans, medicine men and women, sorcerers and witches, could intervene with the forces that controlled the world, and that these people could use magic to make things happen, controlling both the good and the bad in their lives. Scientists of the sixteenth and seventeenth centuries endeavoured to show that the world, and, indeed, the universe, were governed by discernable laws, but this would have little impact on the everyday lives or thoughts of the British and European masses.

Advances in biology and medical theory also did little to sway the prevailing belief. Bloodletting using leeches was the long-standing practice of trying to return the balance of the fluids to equilibrium, thus warding off illness, and remained so despite new and compelling theories about the body's construct. Given the widespread illiteracy and ignorance in society, it was an unshakable set of beliefs and rituals that gave believers a sense of control over things that were seemingly uncontrollable.

two

WHAT IS
WITCHCRAFT?

It is beyond the scope of this book to begin with the archaeological discoveries that have confirmed that the origins of our belief system can be traced back to the Palaeolithic peoples who worshipped a Hunter God and a Fertility Goddess.

What we refer to here as witchcraft dates back to the ancient Celts and Druids, although ever since humans started banding together in groups there have been practices of casting spells in order to harness occult forces; this was originally a nature-based belief wherein people gave reverence to the elements for the animals and vegetables they ate.

The Celts were a force in Britain by 480 BC, and occupied lands stretching from the British Isles to Galatia (modern-day Turkey), controlling most of Central Europe. By 700 BC they had forged themselves into parts of northern Spain. They were a deeply polytheistic people for whom superstitious belief was a way of life, and this belief was gleaned from their surroundings and stories that were passed from generation to generation.

They worshipped both gods and goddesses; their religion was pantheistic, meaning they worshipped many aspects of the 'One Creative Life Source' and honoured the presence of the 'Divine Creator' in all of nature. Like many tribes the world over, they believed in reincarnation. Their priests, judges, teachers, astrologers and healers were known as Druids, and were held in very high command by political leaders because of their power and influence. It took twenty years of intense study to become a Druid. These were the peacemakers, who were able to pass from one warring tribe to another unharmed, and remained in power three centuries after the defeat of the Celts at the hands of the Romans, which had conquered the south-east of England in around AD 43.

The religious beliefs and practices of the Celts grew into what later became known as Paganism, which is a blanket term typically referring to religious traditions that are polytheistic or indigenous. The word 'Pagan' is derived from the Latin word 'Paganus', which encompassed 'country dweller, villager, and rustic'. Paganistic beliefs, blended over the centuries with those of other Indo-European-descended groups, spawned practices such as concocting potions and ointments, casting spells, and performing works of magic. Collectively, these practices became known as witchcraft, performed by a witch. This term comes from the Celtic word 'Wicca', from the Anglo-Saxon word meaning 'to twist or bend', which is derived from the word 'Wicce', which means 'wise', and describes somebody who is believed to have received supernatural powers. The craft has been defined in historical, religious, and mythological contexts as the use of alleged supernatural or magical powers (spells) applied to practices that people believed influenced the mind, body or property of others against their will. Practitioners were referred to as enchantresses, sorcerers, or witches – the pre-scientific judgement of the time.

Belief in witchcraft was (and may still be), in certain respects, the most logical or satisfactory explanation for misfortune or strange events. There were no experts in agriculture, and there were no veterinary surgeons, and whilst there were doctors, there were not enough of them. Moreover, they could not easily be afforded, so where medicine failed to heal, and it seemed that God did not hear prayers, partial hope for recovery could be sought by countering the magic of a witch.

Texts have also described witchcraft as a pact or covenant with the Devil in exchange for the power to do evil and harm others, but all such beliefs began from their association with things such as sickness, shortages of food, bad weather and failed crops. When times were bad, shamans, medicine people, witches and other kinds of magicians would cast spells and perform rituals to harness the power of the gods.

This produced mixed results; witches, who were primarily women, were originally seen as wise healers who could both nurture and destroy; this belief in their power, however, eventually led to fear, and this often forced witches to live as outcasts.

When Christianity became the prevailing religion in Europe, many of the ancient 'pagan' religions still survived, and these included magic-making practices. Subsequently, sorcery came to be associated with heresy and was viewed as evil, but these sorcerers could come in many guises: a professional healer, a midwife, a maker or purveyor of herbal remedies – even a person who was deemed to have made a profit while their neighbours languished in relative squalor. Poverty, misfortune and neighbourhood tensions were leading factors in fuelling accusations and could account for a large percentage of those accused of witchcraft. Sometimes they were condemned simply because they owned land that others wanted.

The *Malleus Maleficarum* (*The Hammer of (the) Witches*) was an infamous witch-hunting treatise used by both Catholics and Protestants. It was written in 1486 by Heinrich Kramer and Jacob Sprenger, inquisitors of the Catholic Church. It asserts that three elements are necessary for witchcraft: the evil-intentioned witch, the help of the Devil, and the permission of God. It outlines how to identify a witch, what makes a woman more likely than a man to be a witch, how to put a witch on trial, and how to punish a witch.

Although witch persecutions were not really in effect until 1563, the use of witchcraft had been deemed as heresy by Pope Innocent VIII in 1484, and from then until around 1750, it is alleged that some 200,000 witches were tortured, burned and hanged across Western Europe.

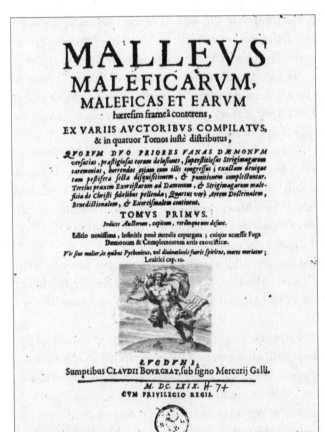

The *Malleus Maleficarum* is a treatise on the prosecution of witches, written in 1486 by Heinrich Kramer, a German Catholic clergyman.

THREE

WITCHES OR
CUNNING FOLK

The English term 'witch' was not exclusively attached to one who consorted with the Devil to carry out his work. There are many misconceptions about witchcraft, but whether it is good (white) or bad (black), it is, on the whole, a religion which admires and gives utmost respect to Mother Nature, and the practitioners of either craft would not cast spells or perform rituals that went against her. 'Evil' or 'black magic' is traditionally referred to as the use of supernatural powers for evil and selfish purposes through association with the Devil. Its underlying ideology is that the knowledge and physical well-being of the practitioner are more important than other concerns, theological or ethical, and it is performed with the intention of harming another being, either as a means of building the practitioner's power or as the goal itself.

In the new world of America, the most famous witch trial was conducted at Salem in Massachusetts in 1692. Witches there were considered to be only the 'black' (evil) type, and fear and hysteria led to trials and executions right across the province. In Britain, witches were no longer the subject of folklore or medieval myths – they were real, and a tangible representation of the Devil. They were held accountable for bad weather, failed crops and diseases of animals and people. In fact, almost anything that could be construed as just rotten luck was attributed to the diabolical acts of witches.

By contrast, 'white magic' was a form of 'personal betterment' magic, where the practitioner attuned himself or herself to the needs of human society and attempted to meet those needs by way of spells to watch over, heal, protect, bless, and to help themselves and those they supported. They intended to take over curses and hexes, reverse evil and protect against any kind of bad enchantment. White magic spells were the same thing as prayers, a vocalisation of what the witch needed, wanted or desired, and removed the middleman (God), focusing on the witch's own personal power, their energy and the energy around them and their will to do good. These spells gave a better daily life, made wishes come true, were protective against the Evil Eye, restored friendships and were extremely powerful spells. Some of the healers and diviners historically accused of witchcraft considered themselves mediators between the mundane and spiritual worlds, roughly equivalent to shamans.

Folk magic was widely popular in Britain in the late medieval and early modern periods. While many individuals knew some charms and magic spells, the professionals – such as charmers, fortune tellers, astrologers and 'cunning folk' – were known to 'possess a broader and deeper knowledge of such techniques and more experience in using them' than the average person who dealt in magic, and it was believed that they embodied, or could work with, supernatural powers, which greatly increased the effectiveness of their business.

The Witchcraft Act of 1542 made no distinction between witches and cunning folk, and prescribed the death penalty for crimes such as using invocations and conjurations to locate treasure or to cast a love spell. The law was, however, repealed in 1547, and for the following few decades the magical practices of the cunning folk remained legal, despite opposition from certain religious authorities. In 1563, Parliament passed a law against 'Conjurations, Enchantments and Witchcrafts', and the death penalty was reserved for those who were believed to have conjured an evil spirit or murdered someone through magical means.

The ensuing witch-hunts largely ignored the cunning folk, and in the Essex records for the period 1560–1603, forty-two 'cunning folk' are mentioned, of which twenty-eight are male and fourteen are female. In answering to charges in connection with witchcraft, two of the women, Margery Skelton of Little Wakering in 1573 and Ursula Kempe of St Osyth in 1582, were found guilty and hanged. Four cunning men were also charged with witchcraft, none of whom were hanged, with two being acquitted. Throughout the early modern period the term 'cunning folk' was also used for practitioners of the craft who were 'white', 'good', or 'unbinding' witches, healers, seers, blessers, wizards, and sorcerers, although the most frequently used terms were 'cunning men' and 'wise men'.

Davy Thurlowe, who was 'strangely taken and greatly tormented,' and whose back had twisted, was visited by Ursula Kempe, who employed a combination of counter-magic, after which he allegedly recovered from his torments. She took his hand and said, "'A good childe howe art thou loden", and so went thrise out of the doores, and euery time when shee came in shee tooke the childe by the hands, and saide, "A good childe howe art thou loden".' Kempe reassured Thurlow, firmly stating, 'I warrant thee I, thy Childe shall doe well enough.' Under examination Grace Thurlowe, Davy's mother and a good friend of Ursula Kempe, told this story to Brian D'Arcy, shortly before she recounted how she and Kempe had fallen out.

In Britain, the 'Cunnan' – 'cunning folk' – were known by a variety of names in different regions, including 'wise men' and 'wise women', 'pellars', 'wizards', 'dyn hysbys', and sometimes 'white witches'. They were most commonly employed to use their magic, charms and spells in order to combat malevolent witchcraft and the curses which these witches had allegedly placed upon people or their animals, or to locate criminals, missing persons or stolen property. They would also earn money fortune-telling, healing, and treasure hunting.

Some cunning folk obtained and used 'Grimoires' – textbooks of sorcery and magic – when they began to be printed in the English language. These tomes were displayed to impress their clients that they were all-knowledgeable, despite the fact that they may never have made any use of the magical rituals contained within them. Such books typically included instructions on how to create magical objects like talismans and amulets, how to perform magical spells, charms and divination, and how to summon or invoke supernatural entities such as angels, spirits and demons. The books themselves were said by some to have been imbued with magical powers.

The cunning folk were often tradesmen and farmers, and as such were usually at least semi-literate and of a higher social position than common labourers. In many cases they continued in their ordinary day-to-day work while earning extra money as a professional cunning man or woman as well as gaining power or social prestige within their community, although there were a few charlatans who later admitted in court that they didn't have powers but were simply pretending that they did in order to fool people for their money.

They operated in quite a competitive market, and their reputations and first impressions were very important. They often worked on their personal promotion: some were known to travel relatively large distances to visit their clients as well as making calls during the night if requested. Some were also known to wear striking costumes or home decorations in order to enhance their reputations as magical individuals. 'Cunning' Murrell, the nineteenth-century cunning man of Hadleigh, wore iron goggles and carried a whalebone umbrella whenever he went out.

The usual method of the cunning folk was to make enquiries into their clients' circumstances and suspicions so they could gain some prior knowledge before they familiarised themselves with their relationships and recent events. If witchcraft was feasible or suspected, it might be diagnosed as the cause of misfortune. Otherwise, they were expected to identify the witch and prescribe action to end the curse. In almost all cases, cunning folk worked either alone, as solitary magical practitioners, or with one other person, such as a spouse or sibling. Although such folk were numerous around the county, and indeed the country, few records were kept because their activities were illegal, and both they and their clients would have been open to prosecution.

Mother Persore of Navestock was reputed to be a white witch, and two surviving records say that in 1566 she was sought out by a woman from Romford to find out who had bewitched her. In the following year, one James Hopkin of Hornchurch went to seek the help of Mother Persore to try to discover who had bewitched his master's cattle. In 1583 a couple from Hornchurch, and in 1588, the wife of a smallholder in rural Romford, were reported as suspected witches.

Miles Blomfield was born in Bury St Edmunds in 1525, and was a man not without means. After taking his medical degree at Cambridge in 1552, he became a licensed physician. He was also a practitioner of white magic and alchemy, and by then was living in Chelmsford, where he employed his knowledge of the art of prophesy and interfered in minor disputes. This ultimately led to him being tried for witchcraft (soothsaying) in 1578, although he was found not guilty.

Elizabeth 'Nelly' Button (née Witherow) was the wife of Zachariah Henry, labourer, and lived in Hockley, where they were married. Button was alleged to have had the power to hypnotise those she disliked so that they lost the use of their limbs. In one story from 1853, a girl who had offended a 'witch' had been immediately struck down by a form of paralysis which defied diagnosis by the doctor. She was left in that state for seven days until Button arrived at the front door and entered without speaking a word. She whispered something in the ear of the sick girl, who, within five minutes, was well again.

Button possessed a diabolical sense of humour and liked nothing better than to drive her victims almost frantic with her occult pranks. Once, when the village blacksmith offended her, she made his concertina play day and night for weeks on end until he became a wreck from lack of sleep.

Another of her victims was a local blacksmith who refused to mend her cooking pot; for a week he couldn't sleep for loud noises that came from the empty forge at night, and his wife's cooking pots would not stay on the stove. She also punished a woman by making the dumplings she was cooking fly up the chimney, which nearly gave the woman a heart attack.

In the end Button met her desserts, for someone remembered that witches could not cross iron and planted a hedge of old knives and scissors around her house so that she was kept a prisoner there. Button was a resident in the Rochford Union house in Rochford, Essex, when she died. She was buried on 27 October 1896 in the churchyard of Hockley church.

Cunning Murrell

Perhaps the most well-known of the 'white' witches is James 'Cunning' Murrell. He was born in Rochford in 1781, the eldest son of Edward and Hannah Murrell (née Dockrell) of Canewdon. His younger brother, Edward, lived in Burnham, and his sister, Hannah, lived in Canewdon with her husband, Daniel Whitwell, to whom James would be a regular visitor. Murrell married Elizabeth Frances Button, the daughter of Edward and Rebecca Button of Hadleigh, at St Olave Church, Bermondsey, on 12 August 1812. They had five children survive out of twenty: Eliza Ann (born in 1818), Matilda (1819), Edward (1824), Louisa Whitwell (1830) and Eleanor (1834). It is impossible to imagine the suffering James and Elizabeth went through with the deaths of most of their children as infants. Elizabeth died on 16 April 1839.

James 'Cunning' Murrell. (Illustration by David Hurrell)

The marriage certificate of James Murrell and Elizabeth Button in 1812. (William Wallworth)

Murrell's first employment was as a surveyor's apprentice in Burnham, and he then moved to London, where he worked as a chemist's assistant. He returned to Essex in 1810 and rented a small cottage owned by James Tyrrell in Hadleigh. It was one of a row of half a dozen or so, in End Way, off Castle Lane, and was rented at a cost of £4 a year. From there, Murrell started his own business as a shoemaker and cobbler. The business did not flourish, however, and in 1813 he had the bailiffs in for owing a year's rent. By this time, however, he was beginning to become well known locally as a white witch, and as such was said to be able to counteract the designs of witches, to stop the evil eye, and to discover thieves and where stolen property was hidden. He also had knowledge of chemistry and was a keen herbalist, animal healer and astrologer.

In his book *The History of Rochford Hundred* (published in 1867), local historian Philip Benton, who had met James Murrell, wrote:

> He supplemented his subsistence by telling fortunes, [and as] a herbalist, administered potions and drugs. He would purchase forty different nostrums at a time, his price being one penny for each, which he refused to have labelled. A sack full of letters were destroyed at his death, but enough remained to prove that an amount of ignorance, credulity, and superstition existed, which appears incredible. Some addressed to him allude to the appearance of apparitions, and from the tenor of others from women, mysteriously alluding to being in trouble, and hearing that he could relieve them, we may suspect him of darker doings.

It was in his record about the history of the parish that the Reverend E.A. Maley, a former rector of Thundersley, wrote that he considered Cunning

Murrell had a reputation for honesty among the local farm workers, with the following illustration:

> Mrs George Cranness was four-score years old, vigorous and alert. In her younger days, while she was at work in the harvest field with her husband, the sickle produced five big warts on her hand which became so painful that she could not continue with her work. She went to Murrell and explained. He asked for a halfpenny from her and chanted a few words which she did not understand. The warts disappeared and never returned.

James spent a lot of his time wandering around Daws Heath and the surrounding woods collecting wild plants and herbs, and the ceilings in his cottage were covered with festoons of drying vegetation he had collected. The writer and journalist Arthur Morrison, who knew Murrell well, described him as:

> a trifle less than five feet high, thin and slight, quick and alert of movement, keen of eye and sharp of face. He made a distinctive figure in the neighbourhood. He wore a blue frock coat, a trifle threadbare, though ornamented with brass buttons, and on his head a hard, glazed hat.

Over the course of time, his name spread across Essex and Kent for his prowess as an animal doctor, and he was in great demand by farmers. In an age where the death of a pig could spell starvation or at the least a very lean winter, the life of one child too many often carried less weight than that of the family's main food supply. Most cunning men were called upon to treat sick animals as often as their human counterparts. Some of Murrell's medicines and remedies were made up in London on the clear instruction that they were on no account to be labelled.

His various nostrums were said not only to cure all diseases, but to assist the lovelorn and even to bring back errant husbands. But it was his astrological knowledge that elevated him to the status of a true 'cunning man', rather than the more usual wizard, conjuror, or hedge witch (loosely believed to be called such because of their work with herbal cures, and the time spent in woodlands looking for the herbs necessary to heal or enchant). Frequently of good education, cunning men (or women) were thought to practise a form of high magic and ritual largely unknown amongst their more lowly peers. Their knowledge of traditional herbal-based medicine was generally extensive and in some cases ran parallel to orthodox medicine. Whether James Murrell had any formal medical training is unknown, but his skill as a herbalist was legendary. Murrell's talents, however, extended far beyond those of simple herbal cures. He had a mirror that had the useful attribute of being able to locate lost or stolen property, while his magic telescope allowed him to see through walls – which came in very useful should an enquirer suspect his wife of unfaithfulness. The copper bracelet he wore on his wrist had perhaps the most useful function of all: the power to detect dishonest men. No doubt it contributed much to Cunning Murrell's material success.

These were by no means the extent of James Murrell's talents. He often referred to himself as the 'Devil's Master' and claimed to be adept at exorcising spirits, lifting curses and chastising witches. His 'witch bottles' were well known and were used in conjunction with nail parings, blood, urine and hair. His success at dealing with witches who worked on the dark side was legendary. One case involved a young girl who barked like a dog and was said to have been cursed by a gypsy woman. Murrell made up a witch bottle filled with his concoction of ingredients, which was heated at midnight until it exploded. The next morning, it is claimed, the girl was cured and the charred body of the gypsy was found face down in her campfire.

George Spearman, keeper of the canteen at Tilbury Fort, had £10 in silver stolen from his place of work, and how it had gone was a mystery as it had been carefully laid in a brown leather bag. The policeman could not help, so Spearman took advice and sought James Murrell, having been assured by a navvy who had a brother who had lost a sovereign. Murrell had used one of his potent spells to compel the thief to return it, and it was conveyed back to the vacant pocket with the thief's own guilty hand.

The next day, Spearman closeted with Murrell at his home. The latter consulted his familiars and told Spearman that the part of the money that was not spent would be returned to him again. Spearman paid a fee, returned home, and stated to certain parties what the cunning man had told him. There he let the matter rest.

A few evenings afterwards, a soldier of the artillery went to the bar to see Spearman, carrying with him an identical bag containing £6 13s of the stolen money, claiming he had found it under the seat in the tap-room. Spearman was delighted of course, and attributed it all to Murrell's powers as a cunning man.

Murrell made his appearance at the canteen, where he became acquainted with a host of other spirits. He solemnly informed the tap-room auditory he had been hard at work for several days and nights upon the thief, and that he had put such a charm or spell upon him, that he could not rest until the remainder of the money was restored. Murrell found himself looked upon in the neighbourhood as more potent than a whole troop of policemen.

Murrell's claim at being adept at exorcising spirits, lifting curses and chastising witches who worked on the dark side, no doubt contributed to him referring to himself as the Devil's Master. His witch bottles were well known – these were iron bottles which were, for many years, forged by Stephen Choppen, a blacksmith of Hadleigh. In these bottles were placed blood, water, fingernails, hair and pins. They were screwed up until airtight and set on fire by means of a 'charm' against witches. They frequently burst, thus signalling success at the destruction of the latter's diabolical influences.

It was always at night when Murrell travelled, often great distances, when he had been asked to exorcise someone. If he suspected that the victim was bewitched then he would prepare one of his famous witch bottles. This was a concoction comprising the urine of the bewitched, together with herbs and pins, which was put into one of his iron bottles. The room would be in total darkness, and the doors locked. The family was instructed to maintain a strict silence, for if they did not, the counter-spell would be broken. It was said that footsteps would soon be heard outside, often followed by furious knocking, and sometimes the voice of the ill-wisher could be heard crying out for them to stop.

From the *Ipswich Journal* of Saturday, 25 September 1858:

One of the most disgraceful scenes that ever occurred in North Essex since the days of Mathew Hopkins, the witch-finder of Manningtree, presented itself at East Thorpe. Emma Brazier, the twenty-two-year-old daughter of a labourer of that parish, had been causing much annoyance by making use of most violent, abusive, and filthy language, under the pretence that she had been bewitched by a neighbour – a Mrs Mole, the 75 year-old wife of a labourer, who together had lived for many years at Hall Farm, and who were both of irreproachable character.

Mrs Mole had been accused by the Brazier family of working marvellous spells upon their live stock, such as causing one of their pigs to climb a cherry tree and help itself to the fruits from the top boughs.

Recourse was had by the girl's parents turning to a cunning man from Copford, named Burrell, who had long borne the name of 'The Wizard of the North,' but the case was so peculiar that it baffled his skills to dissolve the spell.

Their only choice then was to approach a witch doctor named Murrell, who resided in Hadleigh, and he undertook to affect a cure. He gave a bottle of medication, for which he charged 3s. 6d. and promised to pay a visit to the 'old witch' Mrs Mole on the following Monday, to put an end to her subtle arts.

Matters had reached this stage during the temporary absence for a few weeks of the rector, who on his return was deeply pained to find that, after years of earnest labour, such gross ignorance should still exist in his parish that the belief in the bewitchment of the girl and the Satanic agency of an inoffensive old woman was all but universal.

Having visited the girl (and suspecting from her violent conduct that she was insane), the Rector called in the relieving officer of the district, who concurred in thinking that she was unfit to be at liberty, and recommended her removal to the union-house for examination by the parish surgeon, and at the same time gave an order for her admission. However, the overseers of the poor refused to act upon the recommendation, assigning as the reason for such refusal that there was a man coming from Hadleigh who was expected to cure the girl. The rector next sought the advice of the magistrates, and obtained a promise that the police should have an eye upon the neighbourhood.In the meantime, the news of the expected coming of the witch-doctor spread far and wide, and about eight o'clock there could not have been less than 200 people gathered near the cottage of Mrs Mole to witness the supernatural powers of the Hadleigh wizard. Drunkenness and riotous conduct were the characteristics of the meeting, and to protect Mrs Mole from actual violence, the Rector was obliged to mount guard at the cottage door: for, although the proceeding took place immediately before the parish constable's windows (and he had known of the intention for some days previously), he never attempted to disperse the crowd, or took any steps to prevent or put a stop to the disgraceful riot. Ultimately, two of the police made their appearance, and the crowd dispersed. The young woman has since been apprehended for threatening the life of her neighbour, Mrs Mole, and bound over to keep the peace; and we sincerely hope that no more will be heard of this disgraceful affair.

It was said that Murrell was the 'Master of Witches' because he possessed the power to compel any witch to submit to his will. It is known that when one of the witches of Canewdon challenged his authority, he retorted, 'I command you to die', and she 'upped and died.'

Although he was intensely disliked by the gentry, who considered him a dangerous quack and disseminator of superstitious nonsense, it was not unknown for some of them to consult him in secret. To the poor, he remained to the end a valuable member of the community, whose magical powers were always at their service to combat the forces of evil – at a price.

James Murrell foretold his death to the day, and he died on 16 December 1860. He was 79 years old, and was buried on 23 December in an unmarked grave on the east side of St James the Less churchyard beside sixteen of his children. His death certificate gives his occupation as 'Quack Doctor'.

After Murrell's death, the landlord of his cottage buried his chest of magical books and other objects in the garden, but these were later dug up by his only surviving son, Edward 'Buck' Murrell. The contents of the chest survived until 1956, when most of the books and papers were destroyed, thought to be of no further use (although it is said that a few of the local residents possessed one or two of his books). However, before they were destroyed, the novelist Arthur Morrison was able to check the chest and record a description of its contents. There were books on astronomy and astrology, old medical books, and books dealing with conjuration and geomancy, plus original copies of Nicholas Culpeper's books *The English Physician* (1652) and *The Complete Herbal* (1653), both annotated with comments in Murrell's own hand. The large chest that contained the papers was in the possession of the author and authority on Essex folklore and witchcraft, Eric Maple, who passed away in February 1994.

As a footnote, in November 1900, Stephen Choppen, the blacksmith of Hadleigh, was found hanging from a beam in an outbuilding adjoining his

Cunning Murrell lived in one of the cottages in this row in Endway from around 1810 to 1860. St James the Less church (where Murrell was buried in an unmarked grave) is in the background. (Hadleigh & Thundersley Community Archive)

cottage in Hadleigh. He was 69 years old, had retired from work and had staying with him his 8-year-old grandson, William, who found him. A man named George Goodall cut the lifeless body down, and Dr Cosmo Grant pronounced Choppen dead. Police Constable Totterdell reported the facts to the coroner, Mr Edgar Lewis, and at the subsequent inquest, it was stated that the deceased had suffered great pain in the head, which brought about the verdict 'Suicide whilst of unsound mind.'

A Mr and Mrs Shave, local people of Hadleigh, purchased the old cottage in Daws Heath that used to be the Hadleigh bakery in Murrell's day, along with its grounds. The site was levelled, and while the footings for the new building were being dug, several relics were found which included George III and IV copper coins, and an old clay pipe in the shape of the head of Bacchus (the Roman God of wine and debauchery). After being cleaned up, the name 'C Murrell' was seen to be carved inside the bowl.

GEORGE PICKINGILL

George Pickingill was a contemporary of James Murrell. He was born in 1816 in Hockley, the son of Charles and Hannah (also known as Susannah) Pickingill of Canewdon. He had one brother (Peter) and three sisters (Mary Anne, Martha and Catherine) who survived infancy. He spent most of his life as a farm labourer in Canewdon, and had lived in Hawkwell, Eastwood, and Little Wakering, where, according to the 1851 census, he lodged in the household of David Clemens. He also lived for a short time in Gravesend, Kent, where he was married to Sarah Ann Bateman of Tillingham, on 19 May 1856.

Pickingill claimed that he was a direct ancestor of Julia Pickingill, the 'Witch of Brandon' (a village north of Thetford in Norfolk), who was burned at the stake in 1701. He was said by some to have been a hereditary witch, while others considered

A photograph believed to be of George Pickingill of Canewdon.

him to be a cunning man, and he was viewed with fear and awe by the common folk who, with good reason, trod warily in fear of reprisals if they upset him. He supposedly had a wooden whistle with which he could summon the local witches to do his bidding, and his bewitching skills could put a hex upon farm machinery – which he would happily lift for the price of a pint! In a more amicable mood, he was said to be a good wart charmer and would act as a negotiator in village disputes.

Renowned for his ability to control animals, especially horses, it was believed that when he struck a hedgerow with his stick, game animals would run out that could then be caught, killed and eaten. His reputation as an accomplished cunning man grew in Essex and people came to visit him from outside the village of Canewdon, sometimes 'from great distances', in search of magical aid. This was the time when the agricultural village of Canewdon had developed a reputation associating it with witchcraft and magic, and it was often referred to as 'The Witch Country'.

Sarah Ann Pickingill died at the age of 63 on 13 September 1887, and in 1891, George is known to have been living with his married daughter, Mary Ann Wood, and granddaughter, Emily Wood, in Canewdon. Ten years later his sons, Charles Frederick and George, had moved into the family home. By this time Pickingill was in his very senior years and is listed as being on parish relief.

A centenarian notice was placed in the 19 September 1908 edition of the *Essex Newsman*, stating that Frederick Pickingill (George had never revealed his true age and it is believed that he used his son's name to prevent people from finding out) had passed the age of 105 and was hailed as being England's oldest man.

When a pressman called upon him, he reported that he found him busy, brush in hand, tidying up his front room:

He still gets his own meals ready, and fills in odd moments by pottering about in the garden. 'Yes, I'm a hundred and five,' he said. 'And feel good for another twenty years. I was born in Hockley, and I've been in these parts, working on farms, all my life. I only stopped working at ninety.'

The aged man has never seen a railway train. A Press representative took the 'old boy' for a ride round in a motor car, much to his delight. 'I'd like to go to London on it,' he said, 'I've never been to London.' When asked how to live to be 105, he laughed and said, 'You just go on living – that's all.' He still likes his pipe of tobacco and mug of ale (he was certainly not teetotal).

George Pickingill suffered from senile decay and died of heart failure on 10 April 1909 in Canewdon. In the burial entry, George Pickingill's age was at first mentioned as 103 years old, but then later the vicar added notations at the side of the entry and then at the bottom of the page stating that he was born at Hockley in 1816 and was only 93 years old. During his lifetime, he established a total of nine hereditary covens, situated around Norfolk, Essex, Hertfordshire, Sussex and Hampshire.

It is interesting to note how the news of George's longevity and death spread around the world; *The Times* of 12 April 1909 stated that he was 106 years old and *The Star* in New Zealand printed a column about his life which gave his age at death as 107.

Eric Maple, who had first visited Canewdon in 1959 while staying in the area to recover from an illness, noted for his book *The Dark World of Witches* (1962) that George Pickingill (unusually) did not charge for his services, but did receive some money from visitors. His recorded roles included restoring lost property and curing minor ailments, both of which were common practices amongst British cunning folk. Maple described Pickingill as 'a tall, unkempt man, solitary and uncommunicative. He had very long fingernails, and kept his money in a purse of sacking.' He also wrote that George was known to use cursing and malevolent magic on occasions, inspiring fear in the villagers – something that contrasted with the activities of other contemporary cunning folk.

CANEWDON

Tradition states that in the village of Canewdon, where Pickingill was born and spent most of his life, there will always be six witches, three in silk and three in cotton, and that this will be the case so long as the 75ft tower of the church of St Nicholas stands. The dress code suggests that three of the town's witches were of the higher classes, and it was said that, at one time, one was the wife of the local clergyman. Other tales say that should a stone fall from this tower, one of the witches will die. It is also said that if you run three times counter-clockwise round the church you will go back in time. When Halloween comes around, the police are often called in to protect the church from enthusiastic time-travellers and ghost hunters.

Fortunately Canewdon is no longer subject to the vagaries of Pickingill's moods, but the village regularly receives attention from 'ghost hunters' and other psychic investigators. *Most Haunted*, a popular BBC television

Canewdon church. (Author's collection)

programme, based one of its episodes at the church. Most locals, however, seem to think they would have had better luck concentrating their efforts in the car park or the local pub, the Anchor, as most paranormal experiences seem to come from this area.

FOUR

Familiars and Witches' Marks

A 'familiar' or 'familiar spirit' is a supernatural being that helps and supports a witch, and in western culture the stereotypical familiar is the black cat, although a familiar took other common forms such as a dog, an owl or a toad. Being thought of as supernatural beings, familiars were considered to be at least as dangerous as witches because they appeared to be normal animals, and could carry out evil work for their witch without being easily detected. Cats were the most common animal to be associated with witches (and probably still are). Black cats were the most feared, and were considered to be

A late sixteenth-century illustration of a witch feeding her familiars.

Satan's property. During the Middle Ages people senselessly slaughtered cats for no reason other than the belief that they were demons.

The goat connection may be even more significant than the cat; in ancient Greece, the Palentids, a powerful clan, claimed to have been originally descended from a sacred goat. The Norse god Thor drove a great chariot that was pulled by two giant, powerful goats – 'thunder' and 'lightning'. The horned and hoofed Greek goat-god Pan is one of the most important entities of witchcraft. Medieval legend has it that the goat was created by the Devil, and he often appeared with goat's horns, and would sometimes change his shape completely into that of a goat.

Witches were claimed, in some places, to have turned themselves into hares in order to steal milk or food, or destroy crops, but the belief in hares being witches' familiars was because of their characteristics. They are usually solitary and secretive, but occasionally, when they gather in large groups, they can stand up on their hind legs and appear to be in a private conference with one another. The illogical superstition is that a hare or rabbit's paw is meant to bring good luck to whoever carries it about their person.

Perhaps the most favoured familiars were toads. Some of the species had horns on their head, which suggested the Devil, and their spittle was used in some of the ointments used by witches.

In the days of widespread persecution of witches, every witch was believed to have a familiar, and close animal companions were sometimes considered proof that a person was a witch. One of the most common aspects of the trials of people accused of witchcraft was their familiars' need for nourishment,

Cats were the most recognised of witches' familiars.

A seventeenth-century woodcut showing three witches and their familiars.

and although they would sometimes feed them milk and bread, the familiars really required human blood. This was attained from the witch by pricking a place on her body, causing it to bleed, or by sucking the blood out of her body. This inevitably left a blemish on the body which would be identified by witch-hunters as her 'witch's mark'.

The mark took many forms. Sometimes it appeared as a cut or a bruise, but often it was a protrusion from the skin that looked more like an extra nipple. The 'witch's mark' had to be distinguished from a second type of mark, the 'Devil's mark'. Edgar Peel, author of *Trials of the Lancashire Witches*, defined the term as 'the stigmatum acquired by the witch when she bound herself to Satan.' The interrogators, however, accepted that a discoloration of the skin or a sore would suffice for their searches for witches' marks, and even if there was no mark to be found, it was suggested that a witch might have removed it or that it might come and go. This would have happened when the community already believed someone to be guilty, and the searchers would embody that opinion.

In 1681 theologian Henry Hallywell offered an explanation for this in his scientific treatise *Melampronoea: A discourse of the polity and kingdom of darkness together with a solution of the chiefest objections brought against the being of witches*:

Dogs, cats, mice, rabbits, bees – were all named in witch trials. They were supposed to have the most telling names, like 'Suckin', 'Great Dick', 'Fattin', and 'Vinegar Tom', and it was alleged that they lived on human blood from the witch's teats. Such teats, which could have been anything from moles to warts to polyps, were the chief proof that a woman was a witch. It was said that the familiars craved human blood because the little devils were so mightily debauched that their bodies were subject to the continual deflux of particles, and therefore required some nutrient to supply the place of the fugacious atoms.

The witch's mark found a much more prevalent place in the trial records. 'Sathan' the cat normally ate bread and milk, but whenever the witch Elizabeth Francis required a service of him, he needed blood:

> that euery time that he did any thynge for her, she sayde that he required a drop of bloude, which she gaue him by prycking herselfe, sometime in one place and then in another, and where she pricked her selfe there remayned a red spot which was styl to be sene.

In Elizabeth's case, she gave herself witch's marks by pricking herself in several places in order to draw blood as an offering to her cat.

The St Osyth trial placed the emphasis on the familiars sucking blood out of the witches' bodies. Ursula Kempe's four familiars sucked blood, as did Margerie Sammon's toads, and when they searched Agnes Glascock's body, they found what were described as 'a few marks like well-sucked spots.'

Potions and Remedies, Spells and Incantations

Written record of the use of herbs for medical remedies can be traced back over 5,000 years to the Sumerians, who created clay tablets with lists of medical uses for plants such as thyme, laurel and caraway. Ancient Egyptians (1,000 BC) are also known to have used garlic, opium, mint and coriander, and other ancient cultures like India and China also have a long recorded history of herbal medicines.

In medieval Europe, herbal medicines were derived from the Romans and Greeks, who recorded medical uses of over 500 plants. Pedanius Doiscorides was a Greek physician who wrote the five-volume encyclopaedia *De Materia Medica* about herbal medicine between AD 50 and 70. The Celts held seven herbs – St John's Wort, mint, juniper, thyme, elder, willow, nuts and cones – as sacred by virtue of their magical powers.

As the influence of Christianity grew, so did a tension about folk medicine, which was believed to be magical, and had its basis in sources that were not compatible with the Christian faith. The spells and incantations that were used in conjunction with herbs and other remedies had to be separated from the physical remedies and replaced with Christian prayers or devotions. Similarly, the belief and dependence upon the power of herbs needed to be explained through Christianity.

Many monasteries in England created herb gardens for use in the production of herbal cures; the monks made their own preparations and treated the sick in the area adjacent to the monastery. Many books about herbal remedies were produced, one of the most famous being the Welsh *Red Book of Hergest*, which was written shortly after 1382, and contains a collection of herbal remedies associated with Rhiwallon Feddyg, founder of a medical dynasty that lasted over 500 years called The Physicians of Myddfai.

The success of herbal remedies was often ascribed to their action upon the humours within the body. The use of herbs also drew upon the medieval Christian doctrine, a philosophy shared by herbalists from the time of Dioscurides and Galen, from which 'It was reasoned that the Almighty must have set his sign upon the various means of curing disease which he provided.' This meant that these things, be they animal, vegetable or mineral, carried a mark or a 'signature' upon them that gave an indication of their usefulness. For example, Lousewort (*Pedicularis*) was thought to be useful in repelling lice; Spleenwort (*Asplenium*) in treating the spleen; Liverwort (*Marchantiophyta*) in treating the liver; Toothwort (*Dentaria*) in treating tooth ailments; Hedge woundwort to have antiseptic qualities and Lungwort to be useful in treating pulmonary infections (tuberculosis). Herbs and plants such as Mandrake, Datura, Monkshood, Cannabis, Belladonna, Henbane and Hemlock were common ingredients in brews and ointments for medical purposes. Despite hazel being used by witches, witch's hazel was also used to protect against witches. Hazelnuts and hazel wood were believed to protect against fairy bewitchment, and breast-bands made from hazel would be worn on the harnesses of horses.

The Elizabethan period saw great changes in society and culture in England. Men were all-powerful and women had few rights and were expected to obey men. The number of poor dramatically increased and people became far less charitable. The old, poor and unprotected (unmarried or widowed) women needed to be supported, which was a situation resented by other Elizabethans. Up to the Renaissance period, the 'wise women' or 'cunning folk' – the 'white witches' – were seen as helpful, if not invaluable, members of the community. Their knowledge of the healing properties of various plants and herbs was often passed down through the generations, and their role was seen as providing help for people in need. They were clearly distinguished from the 'black' witches, who were described as those who practised the secret arts in order to do physical or practical harm to others. This distinction between 'white' and 'black' witches, however, was lost during the hysteria of the era of the witch-hunts.

The fear associated with witches and witchcraft rapidly increased in Europe, and the Catholic Church included in its definition of witchcraft 'anyone with knowledge of herbs, as those who used herbs for cures did so only through a pact with the Devil, either explicit or implicit.' The penalty of death by burning was meted out to anyone in possession of such herbs, many of which had hallucinogenic effects.

The underlying principle of 'professional' medieval medicine was based on the theory of the four humours (bodily fluids), which were derived from ancient medical works and dominated all western medicine until the nineteenth century. Blood, phlegm, yellow bile and black bile were produced by various organs in the body, and had to be kept in balance for a person to remain healthy. For example, coughing would restore the balance when phlegm built up in the body and caused lung problems, but the balance of humours in humans could be achieved by diet, medicines, and by bloodletting, using leeches, knives and bowls, etc.

Access to doctors and their medicines for people living in villages was minimal, and what few physicians there were stayed mainly in the cities, where they received substantial wages and privileges. Their services were expensive, affordable only by the very wealthy, and as a result, most formal medicine was practised and governed by the Church, which thought illness was divine retribution.

It left folk in the villages having to produce their own cures for most ailments as part of their housekeeping, and herbal healing was of great importance in these early times. Folk medicine relied on the healing properties of plants, flowers, tree bark, superstitious beliefs and mysticisms that were passed down from generation to generation, and these 'collected' remedies were administered by the local healers, 'wise women', or 'witches', in the forms of herbs and potions supported by incantations, spells and other rituals. Healing wells, stones, and charms played a part as well, often in combination.

Herbal medicines were concocted from almost all parts of the herb of flower – the stems, petals, leaves, seeds, oils and roots – and all were individually prepared according to their use. Careful preparation by boiling or grinding broke down the physical structure of the herbs, and they could be eaten in their dry form or given in the form of a tea, mixed with cold water, alcohol, honey, fruit juice or vinegar. In addition, they could be administered as a compress, poultice or as a rub-on oil for penetrating through the skin to draw out infection, and even by inhalation of the vapours.

The folk healers ensured the effectiveness of their cures by planting and harvesting the herbs at the right time, which was at the correct phase of the moon, and the use of narrative charms were said to have been used as way of timing the steps in the preparation process. For example, an eleventh-century book of Anglo-Saxon charms tells us:

Æcerbot ('Field-Remedy') is an Anglo-Saxon charm from the 11th century, which was intended to remedy poorly yielding fields. It consisted of a prayer and a day-long ritual that began at night; four sods were taken from the field, and a poultice, made from yeast, honey, oil and milk mixed with parts of all the good herbs that grew, was applied to the root-mats. The sods were returned to the field before nightfall, when the healer faced the east, where the sun would rise, turning three times clockwise and calling upon the 'holy guardian of the heavenly kingdom' to 'fill the earth,' that the crops would grow. The farmer's plough was then anointed with a 'hallowed' mix of oil, paste, frankincense, salt and fennel, and, to the accompaniment of a charm which began, 'earth, mother of mortals,' the field was then ploughed.

An Old English charm is 'Against a Wen', which is found in the *Lacnunga* (meaning 'Remedies'), a collection of miscellaneous Anglo-Saxon medical texts and prayers from the tenth and eleventh centuries (although some of the material it contains is much older). The charm, which was used to rid oneself of a wen (a cyst or skin blemish), or witch's mark, was written to the wen itself, requesting it to leave. The blemish would then gradually shrink until it disappeared altogether. The 'Nine Herbs Charm' is another of Old English origin, which is recorded in the *Lacnunga*, and was used for the treatment of poison and infection. As its name suggests, a preparation of nine herbs is made: Mucgwyrt (Mugwort), Attorlaðe (Betony), Stune (Lamb's Cress), Wegbrade (Plantain), Mægðe (Mayweed or Matricaria (Chamomile)), Stiðe (Nettle), Wergulu (Crabapple), Fille (Thyme) and Finule (Fennel). Prose instructions are given to sing the charm three times over the above-mentioned herbs, crush them to dust, and to mix them with old soap and the juice of apples. The next step was to make a paste from water and ashes, to add boiled fennel and 'bathe it with beaten egg' – both before and after the prepared salve was applied. The reader was then directed to apply the paste into the mouth of the wounded, into both of their ears, and over the wound itself, prior to the application of the salve.

Wið færstice (meaning 'against a sudden/violent stabbing pain'), from the *Lacnunga* is described as a charm that was intended to cure a sudden twinge or stitch, and possibly rheumatism, that could be due to 'being shot by witches, elves and other spirits that fly through the air.' The remedy was a salve made by 'boiling feverfew, red nettle grown in grain, and plantains, then boiling it all in a bowl of butter. A knife is dipped into the potion and then rubbed against the source of pain.' As with many old Anglo-Saxon charms, physical gestures accompanied the recitation of the text.

THE WITCH'S CUPBOARD

ANGELICA – used to cure respiratory disease and plague – protection from witchcraft.

CORIANDER (*Coriandrum sativum*) – used for ringworm and for a woman to give birth quickly.

CORNFLOWER – used for pain in the mouth.

DEADLY NIGHTSHADE (*Atropa belladonna*) – a poisonous plant used in witchcraft to cure headaches, and also as a painkiller. The plant, called 'Dwale', meaning 'spell' or 'sleeping potion' in medieval times, is also known as the Devil's Herb, so anyone picking the berries had better be prepared to meet the Devil face-to-face.

FENNEL (*Foeniculum vulgare*) – used to cure fever, stomach ailments, insanity and eye disease. When mixed together with St John's Wort and other herbs, it was used in the prevention of witchcraft. It was said to have been chewed by Roman soldiers before battle, as it was believed to build confidence and courage. Fennel would also have been hung over doors on Midsummer's Eve to ward off evil and in keyholes to keep out ghosts.

FIELDWORT (*Gentiana*) – used for an adder's bite, as was *Lilium* (lily), *Petroselinum* (parsley), and *Basilica* (Adderwort).

HEMP (*Chamepithys*) – used for wounds and pains of the innards.

LESSER SPEARWORT (*Aristolochia*) – used to cure blisters and ulcers.

MARJORAM (*Origanum*) – used for gout and liver disease and asthma.

MUGWORT (*Artemisia vulgaris*) – one of the most widely used witch's herbs of all time for its magical protection; it was a cure for flu, parasites, sunstroke and women's diseases. It was also used as protection from fatigue (Roman soldiers were said to have placed it in their footwear to prevent fatigue on long journeys). Mugwort was also used to ward off witchcraft; it was harvested on Midsummer's Day on the Isle of Man (and elsewhere) and oftentimes hung over the door for protection – stemming from the 'protection from witchcraft' superstition.

NETTLE (*Urtica*) – swelling, soreness of limbs, foul or rotten wound.

PERIWINKLE (*Priapisci*) – used for devil sickness, and for any threat of hatred.

ROSEMARY (*Rosmarinus officinalis*) – used to cure wounds, fractures, sprains, coughs, dizziness and stomach aliments, and had a very old reputation for improving memory. It was often associated with wedding ceremonies, and its magical properties offered protection from the evil eye, plague and fairies stealing infants.

ST JOHN'S WORT (*Hypericon*) – used for urination.

Vervain (*Verbena officinalis*) – one of the most sacred Druid herbs, it was commonly used in their many rites and incantations. Taken as a tea, it was beneficial for eczema and other skin eruptions, jaundice, whooping cough, oedema and mastitis. It was also believed to be a kidney and liver cleanser. Externally, it was used for ear infections, rheumatism and wounds.

Wood Dock (*Laptium*) – used for any stiffness to the body.

Wood Betony (*Stachys Officinalis*) – also known as Lousewort – was used against sorcery and ghosts, as well as diseases of the body. When burned on charcoal with Agrimony (Liverwort) and Uncrossing Incense, it was said to reverse jinxes back to those who cast them. Uncrossing Insense was made from genuine herbs and herbal oils that were often used as a coating over a candle so that as the candle burned, it released its 'magic qualities' (much like an insense stick). It was often accompanied by a ritual of 'anti-jinxing' spells.

Note: 'Wort' denotes plants lacking a permanent woody stem that are usually used in combination.

A mixture of hemlock and henbane was applied to relieve aching joints. Headaches could be cured by applying heather in boiled water to the head. A drink made of boiled-down nettles (gathered from a churchyard) was a cure for dropsy, and a mixture of lettuce juice, the gall from a castrated boar, briony, opium, henbane, hemlock juice and vinegar mixed together with wine was used to put patients to sleep (as an anaesthetic) and as a pain reliever.

Due to the rise and influence of the Church and Christianity, folk medicine became outlawed – spells and incantations were replaced by Christian prayers or devotions and the mystical powers of herbs, flowers, plants, trees, gems and other related objects were explained through Christian doctrines. The renaissance of the twelfth century brought a re-awakening and revival in medieval medicine and research via translations of Islamic medicines. As medieval European medicine became more developed, folk medicine with its superstitions and mysticism faded away.

Magic

Magic would only have been discussed in the Middle Ages by educated elites employing the Latin terms *Magia* or *Ars Magica*. Common people spoke of spells, charms, incantations, and the carrying of tokens or amulets, and observed signs or omens. The practices carried out by cunning folk would have included these objects, the properties of which were believed to be both protective and medicinal – to heal injury or disease, to ward off illness, accident or misfortune.

They spoke or chanted their ritualised spells or incantations, which often incorporated elements of prayers or blessings, while carrying with them certain items such as amulets, which were designed to gather magical power, and directed them towards a specific purpose. Brass was used to repel evil spirits and witches, and bells made of this metal were hung around the necks of cattle to protect them from bewitchment. Iron, which was believed to be one of the most reliable charms, would ward off the evil eye, bad luck, danger, evil spirits, and witches. An iron ring worn on the fourth finger was also said to protect a person from what we now call rheumatism. Many gemstones were also believed to protect against witchcraft and the evil eye, such as amber, coral and ruby.

According to English folklore, hanging a wreath of garlic blubs in a house will prevent disease, mint tied around the wrist will ward off disease and infection, wearing bracelets and necklaces of dried peony root will ward off demons, and scattering elder leaves to the four winds will protect you from evil. Some rituals were used daily to prevent and protect people from disease and evil. These were usually performed with the use of herbs, flowers, amulets or other objects that were portrayed to have magical powers.

In the sixteenth and seventeenth centuries, 'witch boxes' became popular wards against witches. They were made up of small wooden boxes which were full of pieces of human bone, herbs, bits of rowan and other odds and ends over which a spell of protection had been cast. Witch-hunters frequently sold witch boxes as they journeyed from village to village, which aided the whipping up of witch hysteria.

SPELLS

The ability to cast a spell was one of the most characteristic traits of a witch. A spell is the word that is used to signify the means to carry out a magical action, and can consist of a set of words, a formula or verse. Used on their own, or as part of a physical ritual, spells were cast by many methods, traditionally by the inscription of runes or sigils (a type of pictorial symbol of a demon or similar entity) on an object to give it magic powers, but there were many other methods that included making wax or clay effigies to which incantations were recited, or the employment of magical herbs.

Spells (or the casting of spells) were performed by working very specific combinations of incantations, various potions, images and implements. A spell has a specific kind of formula, which might use incantations, various potions, images and implements. These elements are designed to gather magical power and direct it towards a specific purpose: to bewitch someone or something, to put into effect some kind of change, or to inject magic into healing remedies or objects. This was done by means of the elaborate and mysterious ceremonies of ritual magic.

Surviving written records of 'whole' magic spells were largely obliterated in many cultures by the success of the major monotheistic religions, Islam, Judaism and Christianity, which label some magic activity as immoral or associated with evil. The vast majority of spells and incantations would not have been written down, but passed on through word of mouth.

Spells would generally be distinguished from magic symbols, words, patterns, recipes, practices and other forms of magic that were not directly exercised by a collection of words. However, some spells were combinations or repetitions of words that were considered to have magic power, but which were not in sentences or verse.

six

THE ACTS
UPON WITCHCRAFT

Magic, sorcery and witchcraft had long been condemned by the Church, whose attitude towards witchcraft was elaborated on in the *Capitulum Episcopi* (later to be titled *Canon Episcopi*) written in about AD 900, which stated that witchcraft and magic did not really exist, and that those who believed in such things 'had been seduced by the Devil in dreams and visions and had relapsed into old pagan errors.'

Pope Innocent VIII.

Until about 1400 it was rare for anyone to be accused of witchcraft, but heresies had become a major problem within the Church by the thirteenth century, and the *Canon Episcopi* received a great deal of attention from historians of the 'witch craze' period as early documentation of the Catholic Church's theological position on the question of witchcraft.

On the request of the German inquisitor Heinrich Kramer, Pope Innocent VIII issued the Papal Bull '*Summis Desiderantes Affectibus*' ('Desiring with supreme ardour') on 5 December 1484, which supported Kramer's investigations against magicians and witches:

It has recently come to our ears, not without great pain to us, that in some parts of upper Germany, as well as in the provinces, cities, territories, regions, and dioceses of Mainz, Koln, Trier, Salzburg, and Bremen, many persons of both sexes, heedless of their own salvation and forsaking the catholic faith, give themselves over to Devils male and female, and by their incantations, charms, and conjurings, and by other abominable superstitions and sortileges, offences, crimes, and misdeeds, ruin and cause to perish the offspring of women, the foal of animals, the products of the earth, the grapes of vines, and the fruits of trees, as well as men and women, cattle and flocks and herds and animals of every kind, vineyards also and orchards, meadows, pastures, harvests, grains and other fruits of the earth; that they afflict and torture with dire pains and anguish, both internal and external, these men, women, cattle, flocks, herds, and animals, and hinder men from begetting and women from conceiving, and prevent all consummation of marriage; that, moreover, they deny with sacrilegious lips the faith they received in holy baptism; and that, at the instigation of the enemy of mankind, they do not fear to commit and perpetrate many other abominable offences and crimes, at the risk of their own souls, to the insult of the divine majesty and to the pernicious example and scandal of multitudes.

We therefore, desiring, as is our duty, to remove all impediments by which in any way the said inquisitors are hindered in the exercise of their office, and to prevent the taint of heretical pravity and of other like evils from spreading their infection to the ruin of others who are innocent, the zeal of religion especially impelling us, in order that the provinces, cities, dioceses, territories, and places aforesaid in the said parts of upper Germany may not be deprived of the office of inquisition which is their due, do hereby decree, by virtue of our apostolic authority, that it shall be permitted to the said inquisitors in these regions to exercise their office of inquisition and to proceed to the correction, imprisonment, and punishment of the aforesaid persons for their said offences and crimes, in all respects and altogether precisely as if the provinces, cities, territories, places, persons, and offences aforesaid were expressly named in the said letter.

The *Malleus Maleficarum* (*The Hammer of (the) Witches*) was published in 1486 by the inquisitors James Sprenger and Heinrich (Henry) Kramer. It would be reprinted thirteen times over forty years despite being technically banned by the Church in 1490.

The book, which was headed by a copy of the Papal Bull of 1484 reprinted in full, was a treatise on the prosecution of witches, and its main objectives were to attempt systematically to refute arguments that claimed that witch-craft, with its Satanic and sexual abominations, did not exist, to discredit those who expressed scepticism about its reality, to claim that witches were more often women than men, and to educate magistrates on the procedures that could find them out and convict them:

> The method of beginning an examination by torture is as follows: First, the jailers prepare the implements of torture, then they strip the prisoner (if it be a woman, she has already been stripped by other women, upright and of good report). This stripping is lest some means of witchcraft may have been sewed into the clothing – such as often, taught by the Devil, they prepare from the bodies of un-baptized infants, [murdered] that they may forfeit salvation. And when the implements of torture have been prepared, the judge, both in person and through other good men zealous in the faith, tries to persuade the prisoner to confess the truth freely; but, if he will not confess, he bid attendants make the prisoner fast to the 'Strappado', or some other implement of torture. The attendants obey forthwith, yet with feigned agitation. Then, at the prayer of some of those present, the prisoner is loosed again and is taken aside and once more persuaded to confess, being led to believe that he will in that case not be put to death.

It was very unlikely that a prisoner so condemned both by witnesses and by proofs would be spared their life even upon confession. The confession itself also had to have been conducted at a different place from where it was extracted from the accused, so it could be confirmed and certified that the confession was not due alone to the force of the torture.

> But, if not even thus he can be brought into terror and to the truth, then the next day or the next but one is to be set for a continuation of the tortures – not a repetition, for it must not be repeated unless new evidences produced.
>
> The judge must then address to the prisoners the following sentence: 'We, the judge, etc., do assign to you, such and such a day for the continu-ation of the tortures, that from your own mouth the truth may be heard, and that the whole may be recorded by the notary.'
>
> And during the interval, before the day assigned, the judge, in person or through approved men, must in the manner above described try to per-suade the prisoner to confess, promising her (if there is aught to be gained by this promise) that her life shall be spared.

Following the publication of the *Malleus Maleficarum*, witches and witchcraft became increasingly accepted as a real and dangerous phenomenon. Pope Leo X followed it with a Papal Bull in 1521 ensuring that the Religious Courts of the Inquisition would execute those convicted of witchcraft.

King Henry VIII enacted the first English law relating to witchcraft in 1542. This provided the death penalty for those who did 'practice or caused to be practiced Conjuration, Enhancement, Witchcraft or Sorcery, to get money or consume any person in his body, members or goods, or to provoke any person to unlawful love.' The act also removed a right known as 'Benefit of Clergy' from those convicted of witchcraft, a legal device that spared anyone from hanging who was able to read a passage from the Bible, which was invariably Psalm 51: '*Miserere mei, Deus, secundum misericordiam tuam*' ('O God, have mercy upon me, according to thine heartfelt mercifulness'). Women acquired the benefit of clergy in 1624, although it was not until 1691 that they were given equal privileges with men in this matter. However, the act brought problems for Henry, with accusations by some that his wife Anne Boleyn was a witch as she had six fingers and a mole on her neck, deformities that were considered the marks of a witch.

Persecutions started and the first trial at Chelmsford took place three years after the passing of the act. The accused, all from Hatfield Peverel, were Elisabeth Francis, Agnes Waterhouse, and Agnes's daughter Joan. The act was repealed in 1547 by Henry's son, King Edward VI, who was more liberally minded about these matters.

A more significant law was enacted against witchcraft by Elizabeth I in 1563, which was more merciful towards those found guilty of witchcraft than its predecessor, the death penalty being demanded only where physical harm had been caused. If no such harm was done to the alleged victim, the accused only faced imprisonment for one year, but at every quarter of the said year should stand openly upon a pillory (in different towns on each occasion) for six hours, and this was deemed sufficient.

Pillorying ensured that the convicted witch would be notorious over a wide area, and it would serve as a warning that a potentially dangerous witch was in the locality. However, should a person or persons be convicted of the same offences again, they would 'suffer pains of death as a felon and shall lose the benefit and privilege of clergy and sanctuary.'

As harsh as the punishments may seem, they were comparatively weaker than the penalties meted out on the Continent. In Scotland, witches were usually strangled at the stake before having their bodies burned, although there are several instances where they were burned alive; in France, witches were almost always burned alive.

In the frenzy of witch hunts that took place during this time in Europe, mostly in German-speaking parts, an estimated 60,000 people were put to death. In mainland Europe and Scotland they were burned, with the peak period between 1580 and 1662 often referred to as 'The Burning Times'.

The first Essex witch trials were recorded in Chelmsford in 1566, and saw Agnes Waterhouse hanged as a witch, but vigilantes and 'lynch mobs' were responsible for deaths of at least 2,000 witches in the 200 years following the Act of 1542. During Elizabeth's reign, 535 indictments on charges of witchcraft were issued and 82 were executed as a result.

It is worth noting that under the Scottish Witchcraft Act of 1563, both the practice of witchcraft and consorting with witches were both capital offences.

Following his accession to the throne in 1603, King James I broadened the Elizabethan act and it became the 'Act against Conjuration, Witchcraft and dealing with evil and wicked spirits', which was committed on 29 March 1604. The changes brought the penalty of death without benefit of clergy to anyone who invoked evil spirits or communed with familiar spirits. This is the statute that was enforced by Mathew Hopkins, the self-styled 'Witch-finder General'. The Witchcraft Act of 1735, passed under King George II, repealed the statute made in the first year of the reign of James I, 'except so much thereof as repeals an act of the fifth year of the reign of Queen Elizabeth', against 'conjurations, enchantments, and witch-crafts,' and to repeal an act passed in the Parliament of Scotland in the ninth Parliament of Queen Mary, entitled, 'Anentis Witchcrafts, and for punishing such persons as pretend to exercise or use any kind of witchcraft, sorcery, inchantment, or conjuration.'

The act provided only for those who pretended to practise witchcraft or use magical powers to call up spirits, or foretell the future, or cast spells, or discover the whereabouts of stolen goods. These were to be punished as vagrants and con artists, and subject to fines and imprisonment of 'one whole year, and once every quarter of that year, made to stand on the pillory on the market day in some market town of the proper county, for one hour'.

This marked a complete reversal in previous attitudes towards the actual crime of witchcraft itself, which was no longer officially recognised as being possible.

New discoveries in science were being made and living standards were vastly improved, thus reducing tensions in rural areas. The last official prosecution of alleged witches was at South Fambridge in around 1750. The accused, a man and a woman, were ordered to undergo the water ordeal. The man floated, and was acquitted, but the woman drowned, and was judged guilty.

By the late seventeenth century, witch trials were reasonably rare occurrences even in the localities where, in the earlier part of that century, the greatest hunts had taken place. Alice Molland became the last witch in England to be sent to the gallows in Exeter in 1684, while in Scotland, Janet Horne was their last witch to meet that fate, in 1722. In July 1692, witchcraft was implicitly reclassified in France as practical superstition and pretended magic (although it did not exclude those accused of being witches from harsh punishments), and was therefore decriminalised. Although a steady decline in witch-hunts was noticed right across Europe, it wasn't until 1782 that the last 'legal' execution of a witch in Europe took place, at Glarus, Switzerland.

The last threatened use of the act against a medium (who had defrauded a widow) was in 1950, and in 1951 the act was repealed with the enactment of the Fraudulent Mediums Act 1951. This included, in substitution for certain provisions of section four of the Vagrancy Act 1824 ('persons purporting to act as spiritualistic mediums or to exercise any powers of telepathy, clairvoyance or other similar powers, or to persons who in purporting so to act or to exercise such powers, use fraudulent devices'), express provision for the punishment of persons who fraudulently purport to act as spiritualistic mediums or to exercise powers of telepathy, clairvoyance or other similar powers.

THE
ASSIZES

The Justices of the Peace, who were judges of the King's Bench Division of the High Court of Justice, made regular journeys across the seven circuits (formerly there were six) of England and Wales, carrying out regulated commissions of peace, of 'Oyer and Terminer' (which was 'to make diligent enquiry into all treasons, felonies, and misdemeanours whatever committed, and to hear and determine according to law'), of jail delivery and of 'Nisi Prius' (a trial before the justices of assizes, held in lieu of the superior court, but in the name of a court).[1]

The Courts of Assize were periodic criminal courts that were traditionally convened at the seat of each county and county borough at four set times each year (namely Epiphany, Easter, Midsummer, and Michaelmas) in the United Kingdom (and countries of the former British Empire). Essex was within the 'rural' circuit, which included Hertfordshire, Kent, Middlesex, Surrey and Sussex. Each circuit court could last up to five weeks, depending on the number of cases to be heard.

The court records, principally those of the assizes and ecclesiastical courts, provided the vast majority of the actual prosecutions for 'black' or 'white' witchcraft at the assizes in Essex. From these records, it is known that between 1560 and 1680 approximately 545 were accused of witchcraft, with two-thirds of these being accused of black witchcraft. Many were imprisoned

---

1   The Assize judges also had particular powers of discretion, namely in their
     exercise of the reprieve system. It was their personal decision after passing a
     death sentence, whether to issue a reprieve and a reduced sentence, such
     as life imprisonment or, from the late 1700s, transportation overseas.

A sixteenth-century courtroom.

or executed, and of the 424 villages in Essex at this time, some 227 of them are known to have been connected in one way or another with prosecutions for witchcraft, which was second only to theft in its frequency. On the occasions that there were sufficient numbers of prisoners in custody for the various felonies, a jail delivery assembly was held (usually in December).

The assizes, along with the quarter sessions, were abolished by the Courts Act 1971 and replaced with the single permanent Crown Court for the most serious of crimes. The more minor offences that were dealt with by Justices of the Peace (in petty sessions) were replaced by the Magistrates' Courts.

The height of the 'witch craze' of 1645–47 was exceptional in the widespread involvement of a witch-finder, although after being brought to trial, the acquittal rate of the accused was over 75 per cent. Nevertheless, against the background of the bloody civil wars (1642–51), which drew men from the villages to fight, possibly never to return, and which meant the requisition of horses, food supplies running short, the blight of plague and sickness, and the further burden of very heavy taxation, it occasionally happened that agitated villagers would take justice into their own hands, fearing that their neighbours had made pacts with the Devil. Vigilantes would go out to execute them as suspected witches for causing the ills of the villages (though it may be safe to assume that these may often have been for other malicious or spiteful reasons).

CHELMSFORD

There has been a court in the town since around 1199, and Shire Hall, situated at the top of the high street, is one of the oldest and most prominent buildings in Chelmsford. It was built to the design of John Johnson, a local architect and Essex County surveyor. It opened in 1791 and features a Portland stone façade. Its use as a courthouse only came to an end on 2 April 2012 with the opening of a new Magistrates Court a short distance away in New Street.

The assizes held at Chelmsford, which was the focal point of the Peasant's Revolt in 1381, were also the scene for numerous trials brought by Mathew Hopkins in the early seventeenth century. Many of the 300 women he was responsible for killing were imprisoned in Chelmsford before being hanged for witchcraft.

The first person to be accused of witchcraft was at the witch trial of 1566, where Justice Southcote and Queen's Attorney Master Gerard heard Elizabeth Francis's confession on 27 July that she charged her familiar, a cat by the incriminating name of 'Sathan', with the task of attacking her victims. The cat was given to Agnes Waterhouse and her daughter Joan. Francis was sent to prison for a year, Agnes was hanged, and Joan was found innocent of all charges.

Shire Hall, Chelmsford. (Author's collection)

An illustration of the public hanging of the three Chelmsford witches Joan
Prentice, Joan Cony and Joan Upney, from an English pamphlet of 1598.

The old Chelmsford Jail in Moulsham Street, 1810.
It was demolished in 1859. (Author's collection)

The second Chelmsford witch trial took place in 1579, at which charges of witchcraft were brought against Elizabeth Francis again. She and several other women were found guilty of witchcraft and hanged.

In 1589 the third witchcraft trial held at Chelmsford was against three women, Joan Prentice, Joan Upney and Joan Cunny. Joan Cunny and her two daughters, Margaret and Avice, from Stisted, Essex, were brought before the summer assizes on charges of witchcraft. The two daughters, having illegitimate children, were most likely seen as outside the norms of Elizabethan society.

EIGHT

Mathew Hopkins –
The Witch-finder General

Mathew Hopkins was born in Wenham, Suffolk, in around 1619, one of six children of John Hopkins, a Puritan clergyman who was the vicar of St John's Church in Great Wenham, and Marie Hopkins.

His education is a mystery; there are no records of him ever attending a school in Essex, yet it was realised from his writings in later life that he could read and write Latin as well as English, and so must have received adequate education, most probably from his father. His knowledge of maritime law was acquired when he worked for a time as a clerk for a ship-owner in Mistley.

The Mistley Thorn Hotel, Mistley. (Nigel Klammer)

Mathew Hopkins, the Witch-finder General.

Hopkins's career in the investigation of witches began in March 1644, after he allegedly overheard various women discussing their meetings with the Devil at the Thorn Inn, which was situated in the centre of Mistley. He is said to have purchased this establishment using some of his recently acquired inheritance money, most likely from his father, who passed away in 1634. An extract from Hopkins' father's last will and testament bears this out:

I first of all doe freely surrender My soule into the hands of Allmighty God, trusting that (I) shal be receved to Mercy onely through the Righteousness & Merritts of the Lorde Jesus Christ my Saviour & I yeald my body to the Earth to be buried accordinge & Where my Executrix shall thinke Moste Meete; & Wheereas I am seised to Mee & My heires of Certayne lands & tenements in fframlingham at the Castle in the County aforesayde. I give & bequeath all My Sayde Lands, & Tenements, unto Marie My welbe-loved Wife & her heires payeing and dischargeing the porcions ensueing bequeathed to my Children; that is to say payinge unto eache of my six Children severally when & so soone as they or eyther off them shall accom-plishe the age of Two and twenty yeares the somme off One hundred Markes of Currant Money of England.

In his pamphlet *The Discovery of Witches* (London, 1647), Mathew Hopkins tells us that he had 'some seven or eight of that horrible sect of Witches' living in his home town of Manningtree, who, with witches from other towns, would every six weeks in the night (always on the Friday night) have their meeting close to his house, and have their solemn sacrifices offered to the Devil. He dared to eavesdrop on one such meeting, where he heard one of the witches speaking to her imps and bidding them go to another witch, who was thereupon apprehended.

Since 1642, the Civil War had been raging throughout the country and Essex was the backbone county for the Roundheads. The anxiety it caused for people in Manningtree, as indeed in other towns and villages, encouraged zealots to take the initiative in the war against evil. For some time, towns-men had believed that strange accidents were the work of witches, and at Christmas 1644 a convulsive illness suffered by the wife of a tailor named John Rivet was the last straw.

Rivet's wife had suffered lameness and an illness of convulsions at Christmas 1644. After consulting a cunning woman, the wife of one 'Hovye' at Hadleigh, Suffolk, Rivet was told that his wife had been cursed by two women who were their near neighbours. Hopkins investigated an elderly, one-legged woman called Elizabeth Clarke (alias Bedingfield), whose mother had been hanged as a witch before her. At his instigation, she was thrown into prison on suspicion of witchcraft. Under Hopkins's interrogation with the aid of Jack Stearne, an unsavoury rascal with a penchant for cruelty, Elizabeth Clarke, after the pain and humiliation of being stripped naked, then searched and poked for witches' marks, 'was found to have three teats about her, which honest women have not.' Here Hopkins had seized on a

passage from King James's *Daemonologie* as a means of detecting witches –
witchcraft meant keeping imps and familiars. 'Witches suckled imps and
familiars, not just to feed them, but more to aggravate a witch's damnation'.

Mathew Hopkins, like other ruthless men before him, quickly found that
he was able to use the prevailing mood of uncertainty, fear and tension to
turn public opinion to his own advantage. As the war raged, the need to
exchange information was perhaps what brought such a diverse group of
people together at the Thorn Inn. Hopkins, it seems, was ideally located
and able to exploit and gain through them, the approbation and support he
needed for the holocaust which followed.

Torture was illegal in England at this time,
and Hopkins's methods were mainly bloodless,
using exhaustion, confusion and solitary confinement to break down his
victims to confess. Elizabeth Clarke
was kept without food or sleep for three
consecutive nights, and on the fourth
night of her ordeal, she weakened and
confessed to being a witch, at the same
time accusing five other women of
witchcraft: Anne West and her daughter Rebecca, Anne Leech, Helen
Clarke and Elizabeth Gooding.
She also confessed to keeping and
nourishing five familiars, Holt (a white
kitten), Jarmara (a fat spaniel), Sack
and Sugar (a black rabbit), Newes
(a polecat), and Vinegar Tom (a long-
legged greyhound with a head like an
ox, broad eyes and a long tail). Rebecca
West gave evidence against her mother
in return for her own reprieve.

As the investigation continued,
Hopkins began rousing his neighbours
to denounce others, and to cope with
the growing demand for his services
he was forced to take on more
assistants. Jack Stearne became his sec-
ond-in-command, Mary 'Goody' Phillips,

Another portrait of Mathew Hopkins.

whose specialty was finding witch marks on the bodies of those accused then joined him, while Edward Parsley and Frances Mills made up the rest of the team.

Together they interviewed and interrogated over 100 people, many of whom were quick to confess under interrogation, and further names of imps and familiars were revealed, names such as Elemanzer, Pyewacket, Peck in the Crown and Grizzel Greedigut, on which Hopkins commented, 'Names that no mortal could invent.' The final number of those accused was thirty-two, with only Elizabeth Gooding refusing to acknowledge her guilt. After being examined by local justices, all were remanded to the county sessions at Chelmsford.

During the subsequent trial before the Rt. Hon. Robert, Earl of Warwick, and several of His Majesty's Justices of the Peace, Hopkins charged Elizabeth Clarke with 'entertaining' evil spirits. On 25 March 1645, he gave the following deposition to the court:

The said Elizabeth forthwith told this informant and one Master Stearne, there present, if they would stay and do the said Elizabeth no hurt, she would call one of her white imps and play with it on her lap. But this informant told her they would not allow it. And they staying there a while longer, the said Elizabeth confessed she had carnal copulation with the Devil for six or seven years; and he would appear to her three or four times a week at her bedside, and go to bed with her and lie with her half a night together, in the shape of a proper gentleman, with a laced band, having the whole proportion of a man. And he would say to her, 'Bessie, I must lie with thee.' And she never did deny him.

After the mishmash of charges and counter-charges, the trials of the accused were held at Chelmsford on 29 July 1645. Robert Rich, the Earl of Warwick, a renowned and venomous Presbyterian, was appointed as the presiding 'President of the Court'. In those troublesome times of rebellion the ordinary assizes had been suspended and special courts had to be set up to deal with the growing witch hysteria. The Chelmsford trials resulted in twenty-nine people being condemned, and Hopkins later commented, 'In our Hundred in Essex, 29 were condemned at once and four brought 25 miles to be hanged at where their Discoverer lives, this for sending the Devil like a Bear to kill him.' Ten of the accused were hanged at Chelmsford and the others were executed in various hamlets and villages throughout the locality, further adding to the witch hysteria.

After the success of the Chelmsford trials, Hopkins quickly became the sought-after expert and charged extortionately for his services, reportedly between £15 and £25 per village. (This was a huge sum of money as the normal person's daily wage was as little as tuppence per day).

Hopkins and Stearne, along with local justices, clergymen and other notable inhabitants, believed they were performing a public service with the witch-hunts. But local country people said that it was Hopkins's personal financial greed that motivated his intentions. Hopkins denied these accusations, stating that, although Stearne and he put themselves at risk with their work, they were welcomed and given 'thanks and recompense.' The records from their actions in Stowmarket alone, however, illustrate that Hopkins was paid £23, plus travelling expenses for his company of witch-hunters, their horses, and for the female assistants Hopkins employed to perform the pricking of suspected witches. Hopkins stated that to cover his fees, he took 20s from each town or village. This was a very high payment when compared with the average countryman's wage of just 6d a day. It was estimated that his fees may have totalled about £1,000. The expense to the local community of Hopkins's and his company's costs were such that in Ipswich a special local tax rate had to be levied in 1645.

Hopkins was well known for his flamboyant style.

Hopkins advertised openly, exploiting the Puritans' hatred of Devil worship and the villagers' fear of witchcraft. This was the time of Puritan dominance; political and religious chaos reigned throughout the period of the English civil wars, and it was with this distraction that Hopkins began to do 'God's work' in cleansing the country of Satan's followers for the second coming of Christ. He had no shortage of business.

He declared himself the 'Witch-finder General', with an alleged special commission from Parliament to rid the country of witches, and began a vicious, county-wide campaign against witches, beginning with the villages of Essex, and investigating every person accused of practising witchcraft.

Fuelled by local superstition and religion, as well as social and personal factors of the accused such as their age, sex and marital status, most witches were brought to trial for inflicting death or disease on livestock and humans, souring milk or causing miscarriage, cursing and hurting children.

These would invariably be elderly, lonely women (often referred to as 'crones'), especially if they had a cat (a familiar). The accused were not defended, and they fitted very closely to people's conventional ideas of what a witch should look like.

Advances in modern medicine could probably explain the majority of these accused as being delusional or suffering from mental illness, the stresses of abject poverty having taken their toll, especially upon those living alone.

Hopkins's modus operandi was to turn gossip and innuendo into formal accusations of witchcraft and Devil worship. In this he was enormously successful, as most villages had at least one old hag rumoured to be a witch. Partly through fear, groups of villagers would act as witnesses for both him and Stearne. His victims, however, were mainly old, poor and the most feeble and defenceless members of the community, or those who were unpopular, against whom others held grievances. He also boasted that he possessed a 'Devil's List', containing a coded list of all the witches in England. He used this list to condemn the innocent, and then used torture to extract a confession from them. He circumvented the laws relating to torture: with his knowledge, he was adept at using his evil ingenuity to disguise the use of torture as 'interrogation', and therefore stayed within the confines of the law.

In the first instance, he would have his victims thrown into an isolated prison cell, stripped naked, beaten, starved and kept from sleep, while using the pain and humiliation of this psychologically against them. If this didn't work, he would use his more brutal and favoured methods of torture, starting with 'pricking'. Pricking was an excruciatingly painful ordeal to endure and involved the use of evil-looking pins, needles and bodkins to pierce the skin, looking for insensitive spots that didn't bleed. If any were found, they would then be interpreted as a mark of the Devil. If none were found, the victim was made to sit cross-legged on a table or stool, then bound in this posture with cords and left alone for up to 24 hours or until such time as the cramps and pain set in. Naked and barefoot, they would then be forced to walk up and down the cold stone floor of the cell without respite until their feet began to blister and bleed.

One of the most favoured methods of torture used by Hopkins was the public spectacle of 'swimming', in which the accused was bound and thrown into water; if they floated they were deemed to be guilty. The idea was based on the belief that as a witch rejected the water of baptism, so the element of water would reject them in turn, and they would float in an unnatural manner. This method of trial had been used for many years, and was given more prominence when advocated as a test of witchcraft guilt by James I in his book *Daemonologie*. As far as can be found, the first record of its use in England was in 1612, when the Northampton witches were thus tested.

Simply throwing someone into a pond or river wasn't Hopkins's style and wouldn't satisfy his sense for spectacle and cruelty. He developed his own method of swimming, in which his victims had to be bound in a special way. Bent double with their arms crossed between their legs, they had their thumbs tied to their big toes. A rope was then tied around their waist and held by a man on either side of the river or pond, this ostensibly to prevent them from drowning. The accused was then lowered from a platform into the water and allowed to sink and rise three times. It obviously depended

The swimming of a suspected witch.

on the dexterity of the men handling the rope as to whether the accused survived or drowned. Many alleged witches died in this way.

Once his victims had been worn down by torture, Hopkins would begin his browbeating sessions, plying the accused with leading questions and demanding to know how they became acquainted with the Devil. All he needed for a confession was a nod or monosyllabic reply, and then he and his assistants would fill in the colourful details. Most of the charges he brought were for bewitching people or their livestock to death, causing illness and lameness, or entertaining spirits or familiars, which usually turned out to be no more than household pets. He was particularly fond of extracting confessions to the effect that the accused had signed a pact with the Devil.

Hopkins followed his success at Chelmsford by creating another sensation in Suffolk. There he discovered that the minister of Brandeston, John Lowes, an old man of 70, 'was nought but a foul witch'. It appears that Lowes had been a quarrelsome old fellow and was sorely disliked by many in his parish. At first he stoutly denied his guilt, but a confession was gained when he was subjected to Hopkins's most approved methods by teams of his watchers who kept him awake for several nights together, and ran him backwards and forwards about his cell until he was out of breath. After a brief rest, they then ran him again. 'And thus they did for several days and nights together, till he was weary of his life and scarce sensible of what he said or did'.

It was in this state of mind that Lowes finally confessed that, 'he had covenanted with the Devil, suckled familiars (Tom, Flo, Bess and Mary) for five years, and had bewitched cattle. He had also caused a ship to sink off Harwich, on a calm sea, with the loss of fourteen lives'. A later pamphlet by John Stearne states that Lowes 'was joyful to see what power his imps had'. Lowes later retracted his confession, but this didn't save him, and since he was not allowed a clergyman to read the burial service for him, he recited it himself on his way to the scaffold on 27 August 1645. As well-documented as the infamous trial at Bury St Edmunds is, it is also perhaps the best illustration of just how the prejudice and hysteria against witches during those times affected even the high courts and justices of the land. No record or suggestion was ever made to check whether a ship had floundered off Harwich.

As Hopkins's reputation grew, so did his ego, and some 200 people were locked up awaiting trial. His name, and his garb of the Puritan tunic and cloak that had become his trademark, conjured up fear among common folk as he continued his evil calling. But his actions, greed, and cruelty were being noticed in high places as well, leading to resistance from judges and local authorities. Some even began to question his alleged commission from Parliament, and as such, a special judicial commission was formed of 'Oyer and Terminer'. Its task was to deal specifically with the backlog of witchcraft trials, and Hopkins was ordered to stop his swimming activities. The commission consisted of Sergeant John Goldbolt, some local justices and two ranting clergymen, Samuel Fairclough and Edward Calamy (the elder). Trials now began in earnest and such was the state of witchcraft hysteria that in quick succession eighteen people were tried and hanged. The sessions, however, were quickly abandoned as the Royalist forces of the rebellion approached Bedford and Cambridge. When they eventually started again, another fifty witches were executed.

With his career as the Witch-finder General firmly established, Hopkins, together with his faithful band of assistants, travelled at break-neck speed, urging on trials with fatal rapidity. By 26 July 1646, he was in Norfolk, where another twenty witches met their fate. In September, he was in Yarmouth by special demand of the authorities, and was recalled there again in December, and who knows how many died as a result. He also visited Ipswich, and shortly afterwards was at Aldeburgh, before moving on to Stowmarket. Along the way, he stopped at King's Lynn, and many other small towns and villages, but wherever he went fear and apprehension followed. No one, it seemed, was beyond his power or reach, as a trail of blood and misery marked his passage through the countryside.

However, time was running out for Hopkins, as he overextended himself in greed and zeal. Towards the end of 1646, the tide began to turn against him. At a time when most people feared him, criticism was launched against him by the courageous efforts of an old country parson, John Gaule, the Vicar of Great Staughton, Huntingdonshire (now part of Cambridgeshire). Hearing that Hopkins was preparing to visit his part of the country, Gaule preached openly against him from the pulpit and started collecting evidence of his excessive methods and use of torture. Hopkins, while incensed, hesitated, and then retaliated with a blistering letter to one of Gaule's parishioners:

My service to your Worship presented. I have this day received a Letter, &c, to come to a Towne called Great Staughton, to search for evil disposed persons, called witches (though I hear your minister is farre against us through ignorance). I intend to come the sooner to heare his singular judgment on the behalfe of such parties; I have known a minister in Suffolke preach as much against their discovery in a Pulpit, and forced to recant it (by the committee) in the same place. I much marvaile such evil members should have any (much more any of the clergy) who should daily preach terrour to convince such offenders, stand up to take their parts, against such as are complainants for the King and suffers themselves, with their families and estates. I intend to give your towne a visit suddenly. I am to come Kimbolton this weeke, and shall bee tenne to one, but I will come to your towne first, but I would certainly know afore, whether your towne affords many sticklers for such cattell, or willing to gave and afford us good welcome and entertainment, as other where I have beene, else I shall wave your Shire (not as yet beginning in any part of it myselfe) and betake me to such places, where I doe, and may persist without controle, but with thanks and recompense. So I humbly take my leave and rest, your servant to be commanded, Mathew Hopkins.

In the meantime, Gaule had published his findings and his condemnation of Hopkins in a book called *Select Cases of Conscience Touching Witches and Witchcraft* (London, 1646). The book was well-written and convincing, and public opinion was aroused against the abuses it exposed:

Every old woman with a wrinkled face, a furrowed brow, a hairy lip, a gobber tooth, a squint eye, a squeaking voice or scolding tongue, having a rugged coat on her back, a skull-cap on her head, a spindle in her hand and a dog or cat by her side, is not only suspect but pronounced for a witch.

Hopkins prudently avoided visiting Great Staughton, but was about to receive his comeuppance. Gaule preached a number of scathing sermons denouncing Hopkins, and then published his sermons in a pamphlet, in which he attacked Hopkins and his accomplices, particularly denouncing his methods of obtaining 'confessions' by means of torture, which, as he pointed out, was actually illegal in England at that time. His complaints helped lead to Hopkins being formally questioned about his methods, after which he retired from witch-hunting and, parting company with his faithful assistants including Stearne, went home to Manningtree, where his infamous career had started. In their fourteen-month 'crusade', Hopkins and Stearne sent to the gallows more people than all the other witch-hunters in the 160 years of persecution in England.

The Fate of Hopkins

William Andrews, a nineteenth-century writer on Essex folklore, wrote in his book *Bygone Essex* (1892), that Hopkins was passing through Suffolk and was himself accused of being a witch. Hopkins,

The hotel has now been taken over by shops. (Nigel Klammer)

Mistley Pond and the church. (Ian Press)

he alleges, was charged with having stolen a book containing a list of all the witches in England, and supposedly obtained the book by means of sorcery. Hopkins pleaded innocent, but an angry mob had formed and he was forced to undergo his own ordeal of swimming. In some accounts he drowned, while others say he floated and was condemned and hanged. However, no records of this trial exist, if ever there was one.

Stearne, who related in his own book A *Confirmation and Discovery of Witch-craft* (London, 1648), provided the answer that Hopkins passed away 'peacefully, after a long sicknesse of a consumption.' There is a record of his death dated 12 August 1647 in the Mistley parish register, which is now to be found in the Essex Record Office branch at Colchester, which suggests that he is indeed buried in the old Mistley churchyard. Today, according to local legend, Hopkins's ghost is said to haunt Mistley pond: an apparition wearing seventeenth-century attire is reportedly seen roaming the vicinity, particularly on Friday nights near to the Witch's Sabbats.

The Chelmsford Witch Trials Ballad

In fifteen hundred and sixty three, we got the witchcraft law,
And then they passed another in sixteen hundred and four,
Between those years in Chelmsford, the witches hanged and burned,
But still the witches cast their spell, the lesson not yet learned,
So in sixteen hundred and seven, at the gallows in Rainsford Lane,
Went a Moulsham witch to justice, Blanche Worman was her name.

She had warts upon her skin, from these she suckled fiends,
And set them onto neighbours and those who once were friends,
Six families they accused her, three goodwives she had cursed,
And three young boys had died through her, their fathers cursed her worse,
She kept her fiends in bottles and consorted with old Nick
Upon the word of neighbours, Blanche Worman died a witch.

Then from Manningtree in Essex, the Witchfinder General came
To bring the scum to justice, Mathew Hopkins was his name,
He rounded up Essex's witches and in sixteen forty five
He hauled the crones to Chelmsford town, they numbered twenty five –
All of them old women, and all mumbling words of fear,
As they went to Chelmsford Shirehouse, their sentences to hear.

From Manningtree in Essex, one Mathew Hopkins came,
To terrorise old women who for some ill luck were blamed.

Mathew charged them with consorting with Lucifer himself,
And cursing harmless neighbours with their ill-gotten spells.
You could spite an ugly neighbour if your bowels began to quake,
Hopkins fetched some hag to Chelmsford to the gallows or the stake
They'd be tested in the millpond to see if they could drown
And if they did they were innocent, for a witch will not sink down!

Most were simpleminded folk, and others were insane
The evidence was flimsy, confessions from fear came.
If a person had the bloody flux, if the bowels had curdled,
They'd drag some hag to Gallows End strapped upon a hurdle
Mathew made her neighbours testify, for they were scared as well,
Then he sent some witch's blackened soul plummeting to Hell!

Now Mathew he is sleeping, but in death he'll find no rest,
For he can hear the weeping of the witches sent to death.
From Manningtree in Essex, one Mathew Hopkins came,
To terrorise old women and condemn them to the flames.

Sarah Hartwell

The Puritan writer Nehemiah Wallington was born in 1598, and lived in Eastcheap, London. A wood turner by trade, he also wrote a prolific number of journals and other textbooks on a broad range of everyday and spiritual concerns. Accounts of incidents included his domestic, working and religious life, and he also wrote on wider issues, about life in seventeenth-century London and an account of skirmishes of the English Civil War. Out of the fifty notebooks Wallington catalogued, only seven survive; one of these contains a shocking account of Hopkins's East Anglia witch-hunts, and how he had uncovered a supposed coven of witches in Manningtree, of which nineteen were hanged. The journals now reside at Tatton Park, Cheshire, where in 2010 a team from Manchester University began the lengthy task of reproducing them in digital form.

CONFESSION
AND TORTURE

The Spanish Inquisitorial System (1478–1834) was based on ancient Roman law. It was different from other court systems because the court actually took part in the process of trying the accused. The Inquisition still remains a controversial and difficult subject because of its association with torture and execution; the extraction of a confession was believed to bring the accused back to the faith, and the torturers were duty-bound to help them. True confessors were forgiven, but they were still required (usually by force) to absolve themselves by performing penances, such as pilgrimages or wearing heavy crosses. Torture, however, was not an infallible method of obtaining the truth: some of the accused were so pusillanimous that at the first twinge of pain they would confess to any crime that was suggested.

The methods of torture varied from non-physical to extremely painful, and often death, and were used primarily to coerce confessions from the accused and perhaps cause them to name their co-conspirators. The torture of witches began swiftly after 1468 in response to the Pope declaring witchcraft to be *'crimen exeptum'*, which thereby removed all the legal limits on the application of torture in cases where evidence was difficult to find. With the publication of the *Malleus Maleficarum* in 1487, the accusations and torture of witches again began to increase, leading to the deaths of thousands.

An Act against Conjurations, Enchantments and Witchcrafts was passed early in the reign of Elizabeth I, which was, in some respects, more merciful towards those found guilty of witchcraft than its predecessor. It provided that anyone who should 'use, practise, or exercise any witchcraft, enchantment, charm, or sorcery, whereby any person shall happen to be killed or destroyed,' was guilty of a felony without benefit of clergy, and was to be put to death.

Witchcraft was closely associated with the female sex, which can be partly attributed to the indirect nature of the violence or destruction attributed to witchcraft, as women were assumed to be inherently predisposed to such acts. James VI of Scotland wrote:

> The reason is easie: for as that sexe is frailer than men is, so it is easier to be intrapped in these grosse snares of the Devill, as was well proved to be true, by the Serpents deceiving of Eve at the beginning, which makes him the homelier with that sex ever since.

It was not directly because of their sex that women were disproportionately accused and convicted of witchcraft. An accusation of witchcraft was only one of many social tools utilised to maintain the status quo by exerting pressure on those perceived to be stepping outside social norms. The expected roles for women were generally more restrictive (passive) than those for men, and it was much more often women rather than men who were perceived to be flouting the norms. Older women were more commonly accused because they were more likely to make small assertions of agency – speaking their minds – which contrasted strongly with the expected female passivity, and being consistent, and appearing to be strong in character, their spoken words would be easily believed.

One of the most commonly held misconceptions is that witches were sentenced to death by burning, and in France, Germany and Switzerland, this was the normal method of execution for them, as well as religious heretics. It was the statutory sentence in Scotland too, but in England, witchcraft was treated as a crime rather than treason against the state or the Church. However, the fear of witchcraft in the counties and districts of England gave way to even more bloody witch hunts than in Scotland, which led to, in almost every case, a hanging, and occasionally this swift justice was meted out vigilante-style by agitated villagers.

The confessions of witches were usually extracted by torture, and everyone from the lowliest peasant to the highest judge of the Spanish Inquisition recognised that under torture, anything may be obtained. However, this presented a dilemma: most people accused of consorting with the Devil were often held on the flimsiest of evidence, and protested their innocence. It took hideous torments for them to say otherwise, and to be offered a second chance at offering a 'free confession' in the hope of winning the mercy of the court. This was coupled with the fact that having been accused of acts of witchcraft, they would be certain to starve, for no person thereafter would give them food or lodgings, and they would be beaten to the limits of the town, and from there banished.

Sleep deprivation was one of the most effective non-physical methods of gaining a confession. The accused was kept awake continuously for days, the induced insomnia causing the mind to cloud and hallucinations to set in. This would weaken the spirit and eventually the will would break. Many confessions were obtained in this way and documented before the accused would be allowed to sleep. This torture caused no physical damage to the body, and from it, countless confessions were extracted and passed on to the authorities so the culprit could finally be allowed to get some sleep. This technique was not limited in the amount of time that could be used, and other suspected witches were often forced to watch the trials and tortures of their fellow accused. Upon witnessing the horrible treatment of their peers, some would confess in order to spare themselves equal treatment.

The extraction of a confession was conducted in secret, often in underground dungeons, but torturous executions were usually carried out in public. Public holidays were often declared and free penances given to spectators, which drew large crowds.

THE BOOT

The victim's legs were placed between two planks of wood and bound together with cords. Between the cords, the torturers placed wedges, which they would violently pound with a large, heavy hammer. Each time a wedge was hammered, an acute portion of the shin bone was shattered. The tormentors could hammer at least a dozen wedges up and down the legs. When the 'boots' were removed, the flesh was destroyed and bone fragments fell to pieces, with some victims even gushing marrow from their crushed legs.

BURNING

In early modern Europe, the most common method of executing accused witches was by burning: the criminal would usually be led to the centre of a wall of sticks and straw and tied to a stake, after which the space between the criminal and the wall would be filled with wood, which concealed the person.

Burning at the stake: a woodcut illustration, 1692.

In Italy and France all witches were burned alive, while elsewhere some were garrotted at the stake – providing that they confessed first. Green logs were used on some occasions so the fire would burn more slowly, prolonging the agony; the suffering could be extended up to two hours. On other occasions, poorly prepared ropes were burned through and the victim broke free, half burned and crazed by pain. One victim in France, Claude Janguillaume, was thrown back into the flames three times before his body was ultimately consumed. Children as young as eleven were sent to the stake, and the offspring of those condemned to the flames were often flogged as they watched their parents burn to death. At the end of the spectacle, the presiding church officials often gorged themselves on a lavish feast – paid for out of the victim's estate.

In Kirkaldy, Scotland, husband and wife Alison and William Coke were burned for being witches. Their estate was sold to pay for their own fate and the Kirkaldy town council paid the remainder of the bill:

For ten loads of coal to burn them – £3. 6s. 8d.
For a tar barrel – 14s.
For the Hangman's rope - 6s.
For the Laird's attendance – 6s.
For the pains of the Executioner – £8.14s., and 16s 4d for his expenses whilst in Kirkaldy.

On 19 November 1626, they were placed in tar barrels and clad only in rough hemp, covered with pitch to facilitate their burning.

THE DUCKING STOOL

This was strictly designed for the punishment of women. It was used for those guilty of prostitution, and some scolds were also punished by this method. It was also seen as a foolproof way of establishing whether or not a suspect was a witch. The fear of drowning alone often brought forth a confession, but sometimes the accused would refuse to confess, and would be tied to the stool and immersed in water, usually the local pond, for two or three minutes at a time.

The ducking stool.

The device was a stool (or chair), which was hung from the end of a free-moving arm that would be swung over the river or pond and then lowered for the ducking to commence. The culprit would be immersed into the water for as long and as often as her sentence directed, although this was ultimately decided by the operator. Therefore, the punishment could last for as little as a few seconds – but in some circumstances the process could be repeated continuously over the course of a day.

Ducking was later carried out without the use of the chair; the victim's right thumb would be bound to their left toe and, with a rope around the waist, the 'witch' was thrown into a river or deep pond. This particular method of ducking was also inflicted on men accused of witchcraft.
It was believed that if the accused were guilty then they would float upon the surface of the water, their body trying to reject God's holy water. If the accused were innocent then they would sink and drown, and this would be proof enough that they were not guilty of being a witch.

The Pillory

The pillory is related to the stock, and was often found in the town markets. It was usually erected on a post, and consisted of hinged wooden boards forming holes through which the head and/or various limbs were inserted. The boards were then locked together to secure the captive. These would be adulterers, forestallers, dice coggers, forgers, cutpurses, liars, and libellers, as well as 'witches'. This public humiliation was one of the most widely used punishments, but on occasion the criminals were maimed or even killed while in the pillory because the crowds would get too violent and pelt the offender with stones, bricks and other dangerous objects.

The pillory also served as a 'whipping post' for the corporal punishment of flagellation, or even permanent mutilation

The pillory at Battlesbridge.
(Steve Hearn)

such as branding or cropping (having an ear cut off, which would then be left as a warning to others). The use of the pillory in England after 1816 was restricted to punishment for perjury or subornation, and was formally abolished as a form of punishment in England and Wales in 1837.

PILLYWINKS

Many unfortunate women were condemned and hanged after undergoing appalling torture. The 'pillywinks' or 'pilnie-winks' (thumb screws) was a simple vice, which was sometimes fitted with protruding studs on the interior surfaces. The victim's thumbs or fingers were placed

A seventeenth-century thumb screw.

in the vice, and as the jaws were drawn together by the turning of the large screw, the fingers were slowly crushed; the studs would puncture the nail beds, inflicting even greater pain. The thumbscrew was also applied to crush prisoners' big toes, and was even used on ears.

Pressing

This replaced an earlier practice of the deliberate starvation of the accused who was refusing to confess to a crime. He or she would be secured lying flat and a board placed over their chest. Heavy weights would then be placed on the board, pressing down until he or she confessed or suffocated.

Pricking

Pricking was more prevalent in England and Scotland than Europe, and professional witch-finders earned a good living from unmasking witches. They travelled from town to town to perform their services, and did not fail to reap a golden harvest. Much of Mathew Hopkins's theories of deduction were based on Devil's marks. A wart or mole or even a flea bite he took to be such a mark, and he used his 'jabbing needle' to see if these marks were insensitive to pain. His 'needle' was a three-inch long spike which retracted into the spring-loaded handle so the unfortunate woman never felt any pain.

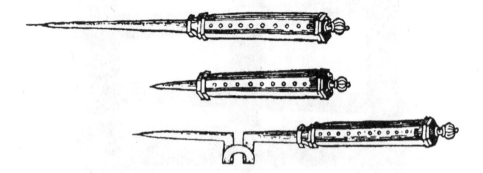

Witch pricking tools. The middle implement, like the one used by Mathew Hopkins, had a hollow shaft.

Specially designed hollow wooden handles with retractable points would give the appearance of an accused witch's flesh being penetrated to the hilt without mark, blood or pain. Other needles have been found with a sharp end and a blunt end, and through sleight of hand, the sharp end could be used on 'normal' flesh, drawing blood and causing pain, which added further evidence against the accused, while the dull end would be used on a supposed Devil's mark.

John Kincaid was a famous witch-pricker who used to strip his victims, bind their hands and feet, and then press his three-inch silver pins into every part of their bodies until, exhausted and rendered speechless, they failed to scream. He would then proclaim that he had found the Devil's mark. Another notorious witch-pricker was John Bain, upon whose unsupported evidence a large number of unfortunate wretches were sentenced to death.

THE RACK

Another method of torture that was associated with the Spanish Inquisition was the rack (or 'Echelle'). The subject would be lying outstretched with his or her hands and feet tied or chained to rollers at one or both ends of the wooden or metal frame. The torturer turned the rollers with a handle, which pulled the chains or ropes in increments and stretched the subject's limb joints, often until they dislocated. If the torturer continued turning the rollers, the arms and legs could be torn completely from the body. It was often the case that being forced to watch the torture was enough to make other accused prisoners confess.

While the accused were on either the Strappado or the rack, their tormentors would often further torture their bodies. This would include heated metal pincers, thumbscrews, boots, or other devices designed to burn, pinch or otherwise mutilate their hands, feet or bodily orifices. Although mutilation was technically forbidden, in 1256 Pope Alexander IV decreed that inquisitors 'could clear each other from any wrongdoing that they might have done during torture sessions.'

THE SCOLD'S BRIDLE

This was used primarily to curb the tongues of talkative women. It consisted of a lockable iron frame that fitted over the head.

Within it, a 'bridle', bit or curb-plate, which was about two inches long and an inch wide, projected into the mouth and pressed down on top of the tongue. The bit was frequently studded with spikes, which could be, through the tightening of the lock, driven partially into, or right through the tongue. The guilty party would be led through the village or town to show the public that they had committed an offence or scolded too often, thus exposing them to ridicule and abuse, with the intention of humiliating them into repenting their actions. It also served as a reminder to the populace of the consequences of any rash action or slander. Although this method was used less frequently than the pillory or stock, the bridle was implemented in the case of witches in an effort to hinder the accused from interacting with the Devil or muttering curses.

Sexual Humiliation

In one such torture, the accused was sat on a pointed metal horse, known as a 'Chevalet', and a variant on it called the 'wooden horse', which was a pyramid-shaped metal frame with a sharp pointed spike running through the middle. The victim was made to straddle the frame and place their full body weight on their genitals, which rested on the point of the spike. Weights would be strung from their feet, causing increased pressure on their genitalia, perineum, or anus.

Another sexual humiliation torture was the seating on red-hot stools in order to ensure the accused would never perform sexual acts with the Devil ever again. In one documented case at Chamonix, France, on 29 April 1592, a woman known as Perronette was forced to sit on a red-hot stool for three minutes before being burned at the stake.

The Spanish Boot

This 'leg-screw', which was used in Scotland, was a steel boot that was placed over the leg of the accused and tightened over a period of many hours. The pressure from the squeezing of the boot would be so violent that sometimes blood would have spurted out from the limbs, and the shin bone would break into pieces. The boots would also be fitted and hammer blows applied to extract a confession, but nonetheless, the heavy impact would shatter the leg bones.

STRAPPADO

This method of torture began with the Spanish Inquisition, as indeed did many others. The victim's hands were first tied behind his or her back and suspended in the air by means of a rope that was looped over a brace in the ceiling of the chamber or attached to a pulley and then to the wrists. The subject would then be raised by their arms, which most likely dislocated both arms from their shoulder sockets. Weights were added to the body to intensify the effect and increase the pain, and sometimes, the torturers would jerk the rope up and down.

THE WITCH'S CHAIR

This infamous instrument of torture contained hundreds of spikes and needles that would pierce the skin of the accused everywhere it touched the chair. While being interrogated, the accused was strapped into the chair and if his or her responses were not deemed satisfactory, the straps would tighten, causing deeper penetration of the skin. It was not, however, limited to witchcraft torture and, despite its name, was a commonly used torture device from the Middle Ages.

BENEFIT OF CLERGY

Prior to the twelfth century, traditional English law courts were jointly presided over by a bishop and a local secular magistrate. In 1166, Henry II established a new system of courts that rendered decisions wholly by royal authority. The assizes touched off a power struggle between the king and Thomas Becket, Archbishop of Canterbury. Becket asserted that these secular courts had no jurisdiction over clergymen because it was the privilege of clergy not to be accused or tried for crime except before an ecclesiastical court. After four of Henry's knights murdered Becket in 1170, public sentiment turned against the king and he was forced to make amends with the Church.

As part of the Compromise of Avranches – Henry's reconciliation with the Catholic Church after the Becket controversy from 1163, Henry was purged of any guilt in Becket's murder. He swore to go on a crusade, and agreed that the secular courts, with few exceptions (high treason being one of them), had no jurisdiction over the clergy.

The use of this exemption from the punishment of death was exercised on the culprit demanding it. It was open to everyone accused before a civil court, as there was no proof of membership of the clergy, but the proof required was that the accused were able to read a passage from the Bible. Few people could read at this time, and secular people who could read would be brought in to oversee the readings. If they couldn't, they would memorise whole psalms to give the impression that they were reading. Knowing Psalm 51:1–4 could save one's neck by transferring one's case from a secular court, where hanging was a likely sentence, to an ecclesiastical court, where both the methods of trial and the sentences given were more lenient. The 'neck verse' was:

> Have mercy upon me, O God, according to thy loving kindness: according
> unto the multitude of thy tender mercies blot out my transgressions.
> Wash me thoroughly from mine iniquity, and cleanse me from my sin.
> For I acknowledge my transgressions: and my sin is ever before me.
> Against thee, thee only, have I sinned, and done this evil in thy sight: that thou
> mightest be justified when thou speakest, and be clear when thou judgest.

Psalm 51 became so popular that it became known as 'the neck verse', as it could save one's neck from the noose.

After being allowed the benefit of clergy, the criminal appeared before an ecclesiastical court, where the sentence even for serious offences would be one of penance. Women acquired the benefit of clergy in 1624, although it was not until 1691 that they were given equal privileges with men in this matter.

THE
ACCUSED

'You shall have no other gods before me': the first of the Ten Commandments was used by Protestantism and its proxy secular institutions to justify the killing of people who possessed supernatural abilities, who were deemed as heretics who had made a pact with the Devil. Their witchcraft was said to be associated with wild satanic rituals, which included naked dancing, and cannibalistic infanticide. The German-speaking lands of Europe, France and Scotland were the hotbeds of witch-hunts until 1645, when England, and most notably the county of Essex, was in the grip of witch fever. In the time of religious strife between Catholics and Protestants, political arguments that led to the Civil War and the subsequent widening of the gap between the rich and the poor, the persecutions of suspected witches went almost without restraint.

In rural communities isolated from the outside world, witches were seldom regarded as benign. In every place and parish, every old woman 'with a wrinkled face, a furrowed brow, a hairy lip, a gobber tooth, a hooked-nose, a squint eye, a squeaking voice, a scolding tongue, having a ragged coat on her back, a skull cap on her head, a spindle in her hand, a dog or cat by her side', was not only suspected, but pronounced for a witch.

It will be noticed, however, that the accusations of witchcraft occurred almost exclusively between neighbours in both towns and villages after the refusal of one neighbour to help another, which was quite an offence in a cooperative society. The one who refused to help was almost always the one who was alleged to have been bewitched. People were also advised not to help anyone suspected of witchcraft, and it seemed that people could easily

The Devil and witches trampling a cross.
(From the *Compendium Maleficarum*, the witch-hunter's manual, 1608)

be fooled into believing the worst about their neighbours. This also served as an opportunity for some to get rid of the ones that they disliked.

The belief in the power of a curse was so strong among communities in Tudor and Stuart England that even the justices of the peace and grand jurymen were instructed that one of the signs of bewitchment was the sudden onset of a disease in a previously healthy person; this was not considered an occurrence of misfortune. Plague had raged through Europe since around 1599, and recurred once every generation until the beginning of the eighteenth century. With nothing known about the root causes of disease, like bacteria and viruses, the outbreak of the 'Great Plague' of 1665–66 was thought by many to have been the work of witches, who were also the primary 'plague-spreaders'.

Over 90 per cent of the accusations made in Essex were made against women, but in many cases, the accusers had to seek the official backing of long-standing local recorded accusations against a particular individual before taking a case of bewitching to court for any real chance of success in a prosecution.

Whatever the truth of the matter, folk tradition condemned witches as servants of the powers of darkness, who had sold their souls to the Devil in exchange for magical powers. They were brought to trial often on the flimsiest

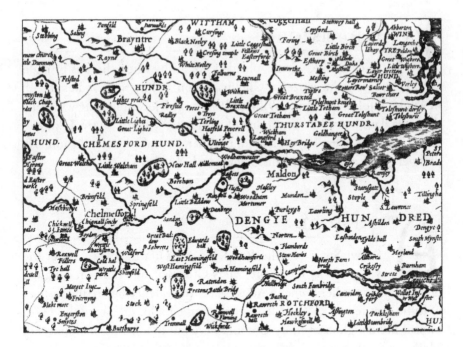

A map of Essex in 1661. (Author's collection)

of evidence and most confessions would have been gained through torture. Today, none of these trials would ever make it to court and would certainly not be taken seriously if they did. The fear of witchcraft did, however, last for many years and one of the latest incidents recorded in Essex involving witchcraft was as late as 1863 in Sible Hedingham.

ABBERTON

Stephen Hugrave, a labourer known for brawling and being a 'sower of discorde' between neighbours, along with Alice Hugrave, a spinster, was indicted at the assizes held at Chelmsford on 18 March 1594 for bewitching a widow, Margaret Stanton.

They were also indicted for bewitching four hogs worth 26s 8d, and eight 'pigges' worth 20s, that belonged to Thomas Clarke (senior), whereby they died. They pleaded not guilty to both charges, and were found not guilty. Stephen Hugrave was also indicted for the charge that on 16 March 1594, he bewitched two cows worth £4, belonging to John Smithe, so that they died. He pleaded not guilty and was found to be so.

ALPHAMSTONE

Alice Buske, widow, pleaded not guilty when she was brought before the assizes at Chelmsford on 24 July 1609, indicted with bewitching John, the son of William Polley, on 5 July, following which he died two days later. The testimony of witnesses William, Mary, John and James Polley, William Rayner and John Miller, was sufficient for the jurors to find her guilty, and they sentenced her to be hanged as a witch.

ALRESFORD

Susan Sparrow, who had lived with her daughter under the same roof as 'Goodwife' Mary Greenleif, and her own daughter of a similar age at her home in Arlesford, gave evidence before the justices at Little Bentley on 25 April 1645, that on one night, she heard the 13- or 14-year-old daughter of Mary Greenleif cry out in a fearful manner, 'Oh Mother, now it comes, oh help me, Mother, it hurts me.' Sparrow said that she called out to Greenleif, 'If your child be asleep, waken it, for if anyone comes by, and hears it making such a moan, they will say that you are suckling your imps upon it.' Greenleif, who already had an ill name in the village, replied, 'I do so indeed, and I will fee with them (her said imps), that they shall suck my daughter one night, and thine on another.'

Sparrow said that on the following night her own daughter cried out in the same manner, and clasped her arms around her mother's neck. She was sweating and very frightened, and shrieking in a terrible manner that she had been nipped and pinched on her thigh. The following morning, Sparrow looked to find the cause of her daughter's pain, and found a black and blue spot as broad and as long as her hand above her daughter's right knee, the discomfort from which lasted for at least a month.

Sparrow also stated that the house she dwelled in with the said Mary was 'haunted' with a leveret (a young hare), which usually sat before the door. She knew that one Anthony Sharlock had an excellent greyhound that had killed many hares, and had heard that a child of the said Anthony was much haunted and troubled, and that its mother suspected Greenleif to be the cause of it. Sparrow went to Sharlock and told him that a leveret did usually come and sit before the door, where she and Greenleife lived, and asked him to bring down his greyhound to see if he could kill the said leveret.

The next day, Sharlock did accordingly bring his greyhound, and coursed it, but whether the dog killed the leveret is not known. However, a short time before it was coursed by a man known as 'Goodman' Merrill's dog. The dog ran at it, but the leveret never stirred, and just when the dog came at it, he skipped over it, turned about, stood still and looked on it. Shortly after that, the dog languished and died.

Sparrow was careful not to claim that the leveret was a familiar, but simply suggested that, 'shee wondered very much to see a Leveret, wilde by nature, to come so frequently and sit openly before the dore in such a familiar way.'

The information from two further informants, Elizabeth Hunt and Priscilla Brigs, taken upon oath before the said justices, said they had been employed to search Greenleif on the suspicion of being a witch. They stated they had:

> found bigges or teates in her secret parts, but were not like emerods [haemorrhoids], nor in those places where women use to be troubled with them; and that they verily beleeve, these teates are sucked by her Impes; for that these Informants have been formerly imployed to search other women suspected for Witchcraft, who have had the like bigges, and have afterwards confessed themselves to be Witches.

Greenleif was asked by the examiner how she came by those teats which were discovered in her secret parts, and she replied:

> She knows not unless she were born with them; but she never knew she had any such until this time, they were found in those parts upon the said search. She also denied that any impe had ever sucked on these teates, but did confess that, 'she hath seen a leveret once fitting before her door within a yard of the threshold; and that she wondered much at it, being about noon time as she remembreth.' She said that she was, 'not guilty of any accusation charged upon her by this Examinant.'

BARKING

Elizabeth Hardinge, spinster, of Barking appeared before the justices at the assizes held at Chelmsford on 6 August 1579, indicted for bewitching twelve chickens on 1 November. She was found guilty and judged according to the form of the Statute of 1563. A second indictment of bewitching Ellen, the wife of John Goode, to her great injury, on 1 August, also brought her a guilty verdict and was judged according to the form of the statute.

Despite the hardships she must have endured from her sentencing, Hardinge was brought before the assizes at Brentwood on 17 March 1580, indicted for bewitching Cecily, the 3-year-old daughter of William Miles, on 3 February, who died on 20 March. Hardinge was found guilty and was remanded in prison at Colchester.

BELCHAMP WALTER

Agnes Dix, a common witch and entrantress, wife of John Dix, labourer, appeared before the assizes at Brentwood on 9 July 1574, indicted for bewitching Ellen, wife of John Potter, on 20 January, who then died. Dix was also indicted for bewitching Richard Hayward on 1 May, following which he languished for fourteen days. Dix was found guilty on the first indictment, but no record has been found of any sentence.

Rose Chapman, of Belchamp Walter, was brought before the justices at Chelmsford on 30 June 1600, indicted with causing the death of John Payne by witchcraft. Evidence was given by the wife of William Payne, who was a labourer of the same place.

BLACK NOTLEY

Margery Wilson, widow, of Black Notley, was brought before the assizes held at the summer session at Brentwood on August 1603, where she pleaded not guilty on three indictments. The first was that on 10 December she bewitched Mary Rust, who languished until 10 March following, when she died. The second was that she bewitched a brown milk cow belonging to Thomas Goodaye, whereof it died on 14 May, and the third was of bewitching Bridget Bruer, 'whereby she was afflicted in divers parts of her body' until 26 July. Wilson was found guilty on all three charges and was hanged as a witch.

BOCKING

Margaret Rooman was indicted at the assizes held at Chelmsford, that on 5 May, she bewitched a black cow worth 40s belonging to Thomas Olmesteede. Rooman was found guilty and sentenced to one year in prison with quarterly sessions of six hours in the pillory.

BOREHAM

Agnes Haven was tried for witchcraft at Boreham on 10 April 1593. She was accused of bewitching Edith Hawes in 'divers parts of her body' on 1 December 1592, whereby she died on 20 December. Haven pleaded not guilty, but was found guilty. She was also found guilty on a second charge, that she bewitched a John Brett, so that he was 'grievously afflicted in divers parts of the body.' Haven was hanged and buried outside the churchyard. A curious fact relating to Agnes Haven is that during the construction of a military airfield nearby in 1944, her grave was accidentally broken open by a bulldozer. Many farmers in the area subsequently suffered poor harvests and damaged crops, which were believed by local people to have been caused by the curse of the witch.

Mary Belstead alias Muldeton, spinster, pleaded not guilty at the assizes held at Chelmsford on 18 March 1594 that on 1 November she bewitched a brown mare worth £3 and four pigs worth 26s 8d that belonged to John Hare, so that they died. Belstead was found guilty and remanded for one year.

BORLEY

At the session rolls at Michaelmas in 1578, Margaret Ganne, alias Welles, and Joan Norfolk, spinsters, of Borley, were indicted with bewitching John Furmyn on 1 March 1578, so that he languished until 1 May, when he died. The jurors said that Welles and Norfolk killed and murdered Furmyn by witchcraft, contrary to the peace, and that evidence would be given by John Bragge, Alice Furmyn, and William Furmyn against Welles at the next assizes. These were held at Chelmsford, where Welles and Norfolk subsequently appeared before Robert Lord Riche, Thomas Myldmaye, and others, and where they pleaded not guilty. The jurors found them both guilty of murdering John Furmyn by witchcraft, while the justice of the peace found them not guilty. No verdict was recorded.

BOXTED

Betty Potter lived in a cottage along Straight Road, Boxted, about 5 miles north of Colchester. In around 1646, 'witch fever' had reached the area, and Betty, an elderly lady, was reputed to have cured the

Straight Road, Boxted, in 1901. (Howard Gilbert)

sick daughter of a wealthy Colchester merchant, for which she was richly rewarded. But she was also accused of bewitching the horses that were pulling a wagonload of wheat south from Rivers Hall (one of the two Boxted manor houses) to the mill at Mile End, towards Colchester.

One night, the son of the Lord of Rivers Hall, along with a gang of locals, seized Betty from her cottage and hanged her from a nearby tree in defiance of Mathew Hopkins, the self-styled Witch-finder General. He was active in the area at the time and was preparing to bring her to trial. Seeking to reclaim the body, he allegedly saw the dead witch come down from the tree and vanish, although all of her clothes were left behind.

Since then, the little dip in the road, which is at the bend at the end of Straight Road, where it meets Boxted Road (close to the A12), has been named locally 'Betty Potter's Dip', and her ghost is said to haunt the tree and the dip at midnight on every 21 October. In 1815, rents from the use of the nearby 'Betty Potter's piece' (field), along with two other fields, were used to establish a charity for the poor. By 1881, the income was being used to support the National School, and in 1919 the piece was sold and the proceeds invested.

B RADWELL

Margaret Lyttelberie of Bradwell-on-Sea was indicted at the assizes held at Witham on 27 July 1584, that she bewitched Elizabeth, wife of John Motte, on 20 December, whereof she languished, sick in body and mind, until 10 February. Lyttelberie was also indicted for bewitching Joan, the daughter of Josias Osborne, on 8 February, who languished in the same manner as Motte, until 7 July. Lyttelberie pleaded not guilty, but was found to be guilty and sentenced according to one year in prison and sessions in the pillory.

B RAINTREE

Alice, wife of Thomas Aylett, shoemaker, of Braintree, was indicted at the assizes held at Chelmsford from 1 August 1589 of being a witch and enchantress of men, as well as of animals and other things.

She was charged with enchanting Susan Parman, who was aged about 6, on 6 March 1579 or 1580, so that she languished until 26 April 1583, at which point she died. She was also indicted for enchanting a boy (who was most likely named Simon) so that he languished from 26 April 1583 until August 1586, when he died. Alice was additionally charged with enchanting Rachel, daughter of William Skynner, on 1 August 1589, so that she 'gravely languished' until 10 November; Margery, daughter of Thomas Egles, at Braintree on 10 August 1589, so that she 'gravely languished' until 1 November; and Henry Joye on 5 November of 1589, so that he 'gravely languished' until 1 December.

Aylett was found guilty by the jurors of slewing and murdering Susan Parman and Simon, and was said to have done so 'by her charms and enchantments, and of her malice aforethought.'

B RENTWOOD

Joan Baker, alias Johnson, and Elizabeth Aylett, spinsters, were indicted at the assizes held at Chelmsford on 30 July 1576, for bewitching Mary, wife of Richard Noke, on 20 November 1568, 'whereby she was afflicted in divers parts of her body until the taking of this Inquisition on 31 July following'. Both were found guilty. Johnson was returned to prison for a year and was pilloried four times and for 6 hours each time to confess her offence. (The bewitched Noke later died on 18 August).

Baker, alias Johnson, answered one further indictment that she bewitched 10-year-old John Welles, whereby he died instantly, on 1 June 1576. The record of the trial is incomplete and the document badly damaged, but Baker was remanded at Colchester Castle.

B URNHAM

Joan and Agnes Thorocke were two local spinsters who were suspected of witchcraft over a series of unexplained deaths between 1578 and 1584. This resulted in an investigation and subsequent charges. Joan Thorocke of Burnham-on-Crouch appeared before Justice Thomas Gawdy and Sergeant Francis Gawdy at the assizes at Witham on 27 July 1584 on charges of murder and of bewitching cattle.

A trial jury of thirteen men were sworn in to hear the evidence: the suspicion of causing the deaths of Jasper Leper on 20 December 1578, Thomas Owgham on 22 December 1583, and Mary, the wife of Isaac Bowles, on 10 February 1584. They were also charged with causing death by bewitching four hogs owned by John Lawe on 1 August 1583, two cows belonging to John Gybbons on 20 January 1584, and three horses belonging to William Leper, the father of Jasper Leper, on 1 July 1584. Thorocke was found guilty on the three counts of murder of people, and not guilty on the counts of killing the animals. Justice Gawdy passed the death sentence and Joan was hanged as a witch.

Thorocke's sister Agnes appeared at the assizes at Chelmsford on 8 March 1585. The trial was again presided over by Justice Gawdy and Sergeant Gawdy, and she was tried for the murder by witchcraft of Mary Bowles, the crime for which Joan had earlier been found guilty. The jury found her not guilty.

C ANEWDON

Few villages in England possess such a long-standing reputation for witchcraft as Canewdon, yet despite the fact that no sensational witch trials took place here (the village wasn't even visited during Mathew Hopkins's witch-hunts), the belief in witches was prevalent here for several generations.

Rose Pye, spinster, of Canewdon, was notorious in the village for being a witch, and she was brought before the assizes at Chelmsford on 25 July 1580, indicted that on 30 June 1580 she bewitched Joan, the 1-year-old daughter of Richard Snow, tailor, of Scaldhurst Farm, whereby she languished until she died on 2 August following. Pye pleaded not guilty and was found not guilty. Despite being acquitted, Rose remained in jail and died there a few months later.

In 1585, 'Goodwife' Cicely Makyn was accused of practising witchcraft and was unable to find five people who would swear that she was not a witch. Makyn was given five years to mend her ways, but did not succeed. Subsequently, she was excommunicated from the Church.

C LACTON

Anne Cate, alias Maiden Head, of Much Holland (now Great Holland), was brought before the assizes at Chelmsford on 9 May 1645, where she confessed to having been a witch for some twenty-two years, and claimed that sometime around 1623 her mother gave her four imps: 'James', 'Prickeare', and 'Robyn', which were in the shape of moles, and 'Sparrow', which was named for its form. These familiar spirits allegedly instructed Cate to 'deny God and Christ, which this Examinant did then assent unto,' and after which she used them freely to maim and murder.

Cate was also alleged to have sent one of her mole imps to 'nip the knee of one Robert Freeman.' The imp lamed Freeman, who died six months later of related injuries. Cate was also alleged to have used the familiars to kill John Tillet, John Rawlins's daughter, George Parby's wife (after her refusal to give Cate a pint of milk), and Samuel Ray's wife, Grace, and their child (who were killed over Mrs Ray's refusal to pay back two pence). Following the evidence given by John Aldarton, Samuel Wray, Frances Trawton, Widow Freeman, George Barney, William Freeman and John Rawlinson, on 27 July, Cate was hanged as a witch at Chelmsford.

John Long, minister of Clacton, gave evidence on 29 April 1645 that Anne Cooper, wife of John Cooper, and daughter of Joan Cooper, allegedly kept three black mole-shaped familiars, 'Wynowe', 'Jeso' and 'Panne', which suckled on the lower parts of her body – a crime for which she was indicted and found guilty.

Long also stated that Cooper had told him she had cursed a colt belonging to William Cottingham, and that the colt had broken its neck after going out of a gate. He also said that Cooper attempted to give her daughter Sara 'an impe in the likenes of a gray kite' to suck on her, and, following a falling-out with Joan Rous, she sent one of her imps to kill her daughter Mary, who was strangely taken sick, and languished for a short time until she died.

It was not for this murder that she was indicted, however. Cooper was indicted for bewitching two children, Mary Knights and James Curstissurre, and was found guilty of causing Mary Knight's death. According to one record, Cooper was found 'dead in gaole.' However, this was likely to have been her 80-year-old mother, Joan, as Anne Cooper appears to have been hanged as a witch in 1645.

Elizabeth Hare, wife of Thomas, appeared before the assizes at Chelmsford on 17 July 1645, indicted after the witness testimony of Roger Hempson and John Knights, which was given upon oath before the justices on 29 April. She was charged with entertaining, employing and feeding a familiar spirit in the form of a squirrel. Hare was also accused by Mary Smith of providing her with two familiar spirits, to which Hare responded by raising her arms to the heaven and exclaiming that if this were so, that God should give her a sign. She begins to shake, quiver and fall to the ground, where she remained in that state. She appears to have been condemned to die as a witch, but reprieved.

Mary Wiles, widow, was brought before the assizes at Chelmsford on 17 July 1645, where she pleaded not guilty to the indictment that she bewitched Anthony, the son of Edward Blowers, on 20 December 1644, whereby he instantly died. Evidence was given by two witnesses, Edward Blowers and Priscilla Briggs, following which Wiles was found guilty and sentenced to be hanged as a witch. A second indictment was for bewitching George Fossett, yeoman, on 3 February, whereby his body was consumed. Despite the witness testimonies of Alexander Byron, Anne Martyn, and one other, Wiles was found not guilty.

She received a third indictment for bewitching Anne, the wife of Michael de Greate, yeoman, on 3 February, who died instantly. Witness testimony was provided by Joseph Longe, Richard Cole, Ellen Mayers, and Elizabeth Hunt. Wiles was found guilty and hanged as a witch.

COGGESHALL

From the diary of Joseph Bufton, a resident of the town, and from an entry in the parish register, it is known that in 1699 the 'widow' Common was reputed to be a witch, and was tried twice for witchcraft. On 13 July she was bound and subjected to 'swimming' in the village pond,

Coggeshall Market Place. The town was granted a market
charter in the thirteenth century. (Allison Bennet)

whereupon she 'did not sink but swim.' She was tried again on 19 July,
and again she did not sink. According to the records of the Reverend James
Boys, vicar of Coggeshall, she was finally pronounced guilty of witchcraft
on 27 December, but died before she could be hanged. The manner of her
death is untold, but it may have been as a result of an illness she contracted
from her trials. She was not allowed a Christian burial.

COLCHESTER

Elizabeth Lowe was indicted at the assizes in Colchester on
21 July 1564, where she pleaded not guilty to bewitching Robert
Wodley so that he languished until 1 May at which point he died. She was
found guilty and pleaded pregnancy. Lowe was also found guilty on the
indictment that she bewitched John Canell, a 3-year-old infant, causing him
to languish and die.

While waiting to be tried on suspicion of practising witchcraft before the
Earl of Warwick at Chelmsford in August 1645, a number of women had
died of fever in the unsanitary dungeons at Colchester Castle. These were
Anne Lamperill, who had been committed by Edward Eltonhead, accused
and suspected of being a witch, on 29 July 1639; Joan Cooper, who died

at 10 a.m. on 7 May 1645; Mary Cooke, who died at 3 p.m. on 29 May; and Rose Hallybread, who died at 2 p.m. on 2 June. An inquisition was held and it was concluded that they all died 'by Divine Visitation' (natural causes). At the end of the trials of twenty-nine women, one was acquitted, and another nine were reprieved due to insubstantial evidence. However, they were remanded in jail until their pardon applications were sent to Parliament, and at least one of them died while waiting.

Colchester Castle. This Norman castle was built on the site of the Roman temple of Claudius. Since the sixteenth century it has been a ruin, a library and a jail for witches. (Michael Jefferies)

A close-up of one of the jail cells at Colchester Castle. (Claire Parfrey)

One of the prison cells at the jail at Colchester Castle, dating from
1727. Prisoners were shackled to the wall, had to pay the jailer for
their stay and food, and were kept in the dark. (Claire Parfrey)

Mathew Hopkins, the Witch-finder General, had persuaded a number
of the suspects to save themselves by turning crown evidence against others.
One such woman was Rebecca Lawford, who had been charged with causing
a woman to miscarry. Hopkins, and his accomplice, John Stearne, had since
moved on to Suffolk to continue their 'crusade', but returned to give evidence
at the trials, as they were witnesses against many of the accused. The nineteen
remaining women were sentenced to be hanged. Four of them were hanged
at Manningtree and the other fifteen women met the same fate at Chelmsford.

Elizabeth Clarke of Manningtree, the first woman accused of witchcraft
by Mathew Hopkins, was helped to a height where the noose could be put
around her neck – she was by this time elderly and had one leg – and then
hanged. She had been broken down by the interrogation methods used by
Hopkins, and named several other women, including Anne Leech, Helen
Clarke, Anne West and her daughter Rebecca, who confessed and implicated
her mother and others, thus saving herself from hanging.

Margaret Moone was indicted for bewitching John, the young son of
Richard Edwards of Manningtree on 25 June, whereby he died on 5 July.
This crime was allegedly co-committed with Anne West and Anne Leech.
Moone was also found guilty of having:

...bewitched a brown cow that belonged to Thomas Cooker, and the malefic murder of Joan Cornwall. Margaret vehemently denied every particular made against her, and on her way to the gallows she collapsed and died; she had proclaimed on several occasions that the Devil often told her she would never be hanged.

COLNE ENGAINE

Anne Crabbe, spinster, was indicted at the assizes held at Chelmsford on 19 February 1590 that on 24 July 1589 she bewitched Ellen Leppingwell so that her right leg 'did rott off'. Anne pleaded not guilty, but was found guilty, and judged according to the form of the statute.

CREEKSEA

Mary Sadler was born in Burnham in 1826, the daughter (and eldest of seven siblings) of William Sadler, a fisherman of Creeksea, and Jane Perry, and the family lived at Ferry Cottage, Creeksea. Sadler was 22 years old when she married William Cockley, a coal porter of Tollesbury, in 1848 in Maldon, and they lived in Burnham. They had eight children: Daniel (who died aged just 3 in 1853), William, Louisa, Elizabeth, Harriet, John, Frederick and Sophia Eliza. William Cockley died aged 65 in 1878, and Mary remained a widow for twenty-seven years, later living on High Street, Burnham, and then moving back to Creeksea, where she lived in Burnham Road, at around the turn of the century, until her death in 1905 at the age of 81.

Eric Maple had an article, *The Witches of Dengie*, published in the Autumn 1962 issue of *The Folklore*, Volume 73, in which he mentioned the witch Mary Cockley of Ostend, near Burnham-on-Crouch, whom he had learned about from an interview with a Mr Playle, who remembered Cockley when he was a boy:

In the year 1960 I completed an investigation of the witchcraft traditions of the Dengie Hundred of South-East Essex. Several other villages of the Hundred boasted their witches towards the close of the last century.

At Ostend, near Burnham-on-Crouch, lived Mary Cockley, a woman who was feared for her power of ill wishing. Mr Playle of this village remembers how as a boy he refused to run an errand for her and was threatened with: 'You'll come home wetter than when you set out!' In fact he fell into a pond and almost drowned.

On returning home he was met by the jeers of the witch which so enraged his mother that she struck her with a house flannel. His mother was immediately taken ill, but whether from an evil spell or merely the effect of terror Mr Playle cannot be sure.

DAGENHAM

Joan Upney was brought before Sir Henry Gray Knight at Chelmsford on 3 May 1589, indicted for bewitching Joan Harwood on 27 March, whereby she died on 24 August. She pleaded not guilty, confessing that while her eldest daughter "would neuer abide to meddle with her toades,' meaning that she refused to participate in witchcraft, her youngest daughter 'would handle them, and use them as well as her selfe' – suggesting that she was a practising witch.

Upney had run away after she had heard that John Harrolde and Richard Foster accused her of being a witch, because she had been examined in 1584, where she confessed to sending her familiar toad to pinch and suck at John Harrolde's wife until she died. Upney confessed that she had been given a familiar like a mole by Fustian Kirtle (alias 'Mother' Arnold), a witch of Barking, who told her that if she wanted to do ill to anyone, to send the familiar and it would clap them. After the death of this familiar, 'Mother' Arnold provided Upney two more familiars: 'another moule and a toad, which she kept a great while.' Upney was found guilty and was judged according to the statute. She died very penitent, 'asking God and the world for forgivenes, even to her last gasp, for her wicked and detestable life.'

Richard Foster had appeared at the assizes at Chelmsford as a witness before. In 1591, he accused Agnes Whitland, spinster, of bewitching one of his sows worth 10s, on 10 July, so that it died, but she was found not guilty. She was also indicted for bewitching a 'sorrell' mare worth £3 6s 8d, and a 'yellow donne' cow worth 40s that belonged to John Collopp, on 30 April, for which she was found guilty and was sentenced to one year in Colchester jail.

Whitland was further indicted at the same session for bewitching the infant William Greene on 13 July, and at other times, whereby he died on 29 July, and also of bewitching Margaret, the 4-year-old daughter of John Collopp, on 26 December, who died on 4 January. She was found not guilty on those charges, and was sentenced to one year in Colchester jail.

Helen Graye, spinster, was hanged for bewitching three of her neighbours, two of whom died. She was brought before the assizes at Chelmsford in 1591, and was found guilty on the following indictments: that on 12 February, she bewitched Anne Bixon, whereby she died on 30 March. On 7 March, she bewitched 'foure gallond of Creame' that belonged to John Horold, so that butter could not be made of it. She was also found guilty of having bewitched Ellen Playt on 28 March, whereby she languished, and continued to do so. Graye was also found guilty of bewitching a cow worth 32s 4d that belonged to Henry Whood on 11 September, so that it died, and of bewitching Richard Foster in his body on 22 October.

DANBURY

John Smythe, alias Samond, a beer-brewer and known common enchanter and witch, was brought before the assizes held at Chelmsford on 4 July 1560, indicted for bewitching John Grant, Bridget Pecocke and Anthony Graunte, with the intention of killing them, on various days before and since 28 May, so that Pecocke languished from that day until 29 August, when she died, and Anthony languished from 8 May until 29 May, when he died. The verdict was not recorded.

Smythe appeared again at Chelmsford on 2 March 1570, indicted for stealing eleven sheep from 'Bycknaker Common' on 3 November 1568, ten sheep worth 4s each that belonged to Simon Hoode, and of stealing ten lambs worth 2s 6d each that belonged to Henry Bredges, on 21 November 1569. He was found guilty, and was sent to Colchester jail.

Smythe, alias Salmon, faced another trial at Chelmsford on 28 August 1572, where he was found guilty of bewitching two cows worth £4 belonging to William Treasure on 26 January, so that each of them died. The verdict was not recorded.

Another appearance was before the Essex Quarter Sessions, where he was found guilty of bewitching eight cows, six calves, three pigs and seven ewes belonging to Francis Simon of Stow Maries. The sentence was not recorded, but he was, however, acquitted on a second charge of bewitching to death Rose Larkin also of Stow Maries.

The last recorded indictment of John Smythe, alias Salmon, was at the assizes held at Chelmsford on 13 March 1587, where he was tried and found not guilty of bewitching Rose Larkyn, of Stow Maries, on 6 November 1586, who died five days later.

EAST MERSEA

Joan Colson, spinster, was brought before the assizes held at Witham on 27 July 1584, where she pleaded not guilty to two indictments of murder by witchcraft. Colson allegedly bewitched Richard, the son of Richard Kennett, at East Mersea on 30 June, whereby he died on 20 August. She was also alleged to have bewitched John, son of Richard Wager, on 12 January, whereby he languished until 10 March, when he died. Colson was found guilty and remanded.

The grave of Sarah Wrench (1833–1848) by the north wall of the chancel at St Edmund's Church is unusual for an English grave because it is covered by a mortsafe: a protective cage. Popular speculation is that the cage was designed to keep her from escaping her grave after death. However, the East Mersea parish records say that Wrench was 15 years old when she was buried by the curate Nathaniel Forster on 10 May 1848.

ELSENHAM

Agnes Berden of Elsenham, spinster, and a common enchantress and witch, was brought before Lord Robert Ryche, Sir Thomas Myldmay, Thomas Mead and Henry Capell at the assizes held at Chelmsford on 30 July 1576, indicted for exercising the 'diabolical and cunning art of bewitchment and enchantment, of not having God before her eyes, but being seduced by diabolical instigation, and for most cunningly enchanting out of her malice Thomas Barlee gentleman, being aged one and a half years', so that he languished for three days, after which his body was so 'vexed and troubled' that his life was determined to be essentially 'disposed of'.

FEERING

Lucy Fyssher, spinster, was brought before the assizes held at Chelmsford on 2 March 1584, indicted for two murders by witchcraft. She allegedly bewitched John Ballerd on 1 February, whereby he languished until he died on 14 February, and she did the same to John Dyes on 24 August, whereby he languishes to the day of the trial. Fyssher was found guilty.

At the assizes held at Chelmsford on 23 July 1601, Margaret Smithe gave evidence against Anne Harris, who was indicted for bewitching Mary Smyth on 10 May, who died ten days later. Harris was found guilty and hanged.

F ELSTEAD

Alice Alberte, spinster, appeared before the assizes held at Chelmsford on 28 March 1593 on an indictment that on 25 July 1592, she bewitched twenty-two sheep worth £5, a cow worth 40s, a calf worth 8s, and a pig worth 8s, belonging to Roger Wood. Despite her plea of not guilty, she was judged according to the form of the statute, and was delivered to Colchester jail.

G OSFIELD

Elizabeth Garrett and Joan Garrett, spinsters, were indicted for bewitching Ralph Huntman on 26 December, who died two days later, and for bewitching Walsingham Cooke on 31 December, whereby 'he was grieviously [sic] vexed in divers parts of his body' for a long time. They were both found guilty on the first indictment, and Joan was remanded for one year. Elizabeth was also found guilty on the second indictment, but Joan was found not guilty.

G REAT BURSTEAD

Agnes Bryant, spinster, was brought before the assizes at Chelmsford on 2 August 1582 to answer the charge that on 23 April, she bewitched Daniel Fynche, who died on 5 May. She also had to answer a second charge of bewitching twenty 'brewinges of beere' belonging to Gabrief Bee on 20 October, and at other times, by reason of which the beer 'wolde not worke and sporge', and also of bewitching a gelding belonging to John Atkynsome, which died on 29 March. Bryant pleaded not guilty, but was found guilty on all three indictments.

G REAT DUNMOW

Alice, the wife of John Prestmarye, pleaded not guilty at the assizes held at Brentwood on 13 March 1567 to bewitching Edward, the son of Robert Parker, tanner, on 1 February, thus putting him in peril of his life, so that his life was despaired of. She was found guilty and was imprisoned in Colchester jail for suspicion of witchcraft.

Alice Prestmarye was brought before the assizes at Brentwood again on 14 July 1578, where she was found guilty of bewitching two cows and three calves that belonged to Nicholas Whale on 1 March. Prestmarye's husband, John, committed suicide before his wife's trial. It is assumed that he would have been made to provide evidence against his wife, and so hanged himself from a walnut tree in his garden.

Joan Prestmary and her husband, Richard, were indicted for bewitching Gabriel Smythe, bricklayer, on 10 January 1579, whereby he languished until he died on 17 July. Both pleaded not guilty at the assizes held at Chelmsford on 6 August 1579, but were found guilty, and sentenced to hanging.

Agnes Draper, spinster, was brought before the assizes held at Chelmsford on 10 July 1592, indicted for bewitching Alice, the wife of William Handley on 1 July, whereby she lost the use of the upper part of her body. Draper was found guilty and remanded for one year.

Andrea Mathewe, spinster, appeared before the assizes at Chelmsford on 10 July 1592, on the indictment that on 1 January she bewitched a cow and a calf belonging to Henry Longe, gentleman, whereby they died. She was found guilty, and judged according to the form of the statute.

Andrea may well be the Audrey Mathewe who appeared at the assizes held at Brentwood on 8 August 1594, and was found guilty on the indictment that on 20 August 1593 she bewitched Robert Underwood, whereby he died on 16 February. She was also found guilty of bewitching Rebecca, the daughter of George Gynne, on 10 December, whereby she died on 28 January.

GREAT LEIGHS

Elizabeth Brooke was brought before the assizes held at Chelmsford on 2 March 1584, charged with bewitching Margaret, the wife of John Cleveland, on 1 June, whereby she died nine days later. Brookes was found guilty, and was further indicted for bewitching and causing the death of animals: six cows and six horses and mares that belonged to James Holmestead, as well as a cow, four heifers and four pigs worth £10 that belonged to another unnamed farmer, two cows and two mares worth £5 belonging to Thomas Cornyshe, and several sows worth 40s of a 'George', so that they died.

At the assizes held at Chelmsford on 12 March 1621, Anne Hewghes was brought before the jurors on three indictments. The first was that on 24 June she bewitched John Archer, who died on the same day. Witnesses John Steele, Mris Buckle, Rich Oddin, Anne Kent and William Wallis all gave evidence against Hewghes. The second indictment was for bewitching Margaret Bright on 1 February, whereby her body was consumed. The third indictment was for bewitching Thomas Meade on 1 August, whereby his body was consumed. The jury found her not guilty on all three counts, and she was acquitted.

For many years the ghost of Anne Hewghes was said to have haunted St Anne's Castle Inn at Little Waltham: Hewghes reputedly murdered her husband by witchcraft and was then burned as a witch for the crime in 1621.

GREAT SAMPFORD

Rose Clarens, spinster, was found guilty on the indictment that in 1587 she bewitched two boars worth 10s that belonged to Richard Bakers, and which died as a consequence on 31 March. Clarens was also found guilty of bewitching a horse, a cow and a pig worth 4s, belonging to Thomas Onyon, on 31 May. She was again found guilty and was remanded for a year.

GREAT WALTHAM

Elizabeth, wife of John Lowys, husbandman, was the first person indicted for murder by witchcraft to be prosecuted under the new statute 'Act agaynst Conjurations, Enchantments and Witchcrafts' which opened the way for the period of intense witchcraft persecution that affected England for the rest of the sixteenth century and well into the seventeenth century.

At the assizes held at Colchester on 21 July 1564, Lowys was indicted for bewitching John Wodley, aged 3 months, on 15 April, so that he languished and died the following day. She was also indicted that on 25 April she bewitched Robert Wodely, husbandman, and the infant's father, so that he died on 1 May. A third indictment was that on 20 April she bewitched John, the son of Gregory Canall, yeoman, so that he died on 1 May. Lowys pleaded not guilty, but after being judged guilty on all counts, pleaded her pregnancy. She was imprisoned and remanded in custody on 30 March 1565, pending inspection by a jury of matrons. They decided that she was not pregnant, and Lowys was hanged.

Ellen, wife of John Bett of Much (Great) Waltham, was indicted at the assizes held at Chelmsford on 3 July 1589, for bewitching Margery, wife of William Baulderson, on 20 October, whereby she died. Bett was found guilty, and remanded without judgement. Bett was also indicted for bewitching Anne Manning on 20 May, who languished until she died on 29 November. Bett pleaded not guilty but was remanded without judgement. It is quite likely that, having been found guilty of two murders, Bett was hanged.

HADLEIGH

Elizabeth Eves, the 'witch of Hadleigh', was held responsible for all the unexplained disasters of the village, from sickness in pigs to the blighting of fruit crops, and was a witch against whom James Murrell, the cunning man of Hadleigh, pitched all the powers of white magic.

Born Elizabeth Finch in 1796 at Sible Hedingham, she was the daughter of Joseph Finch and Martha Coney. She married Adam Finch (presumably a cousin) on 19 June 1822, and then William Eves, an agricultural farmer, and they lived in Hadleigh from around 1836 until her death in 1869.

Elizabeth's son, Joseph, was born around 1826 and a daughter, Eliza, was born in 1834 in Belchamps Walter, but was baptised in Hadleigh in 1837. A curiosity is that from the records of 1837 and 1841, Elizabeth and William were living together as a couple, but although she went by the name of Elizabeth Eves, they did not marry until 5 July 1843 at Hadleigh, the record of which shows that she was a widow.

In 1861, William and Elizabeth Eves were living at On Causeway, Hadleigh, and their daughter and her husband lived with them.

Elizabeth Eves died in early 1869. She was 71 years old, and it was after her death that a curious and macabre story was circulated around the village, which was included in the book *The Dark World of Witches* by Eric Maple in 1962:

When the witch died, nobody could be found to lay out the body, but finally one woman agreed to do this provided she was not left alone with the corpse. She and a neighbour then hurried through their task and were about to leave when a man entered the room. It was the witch's son, who had been away from home for a long time. His first words were, 'I know my mother is dead. Her spirit came and stood at my side as I worked in the fields.' He then asked the women not to leave as he had one last task for them.

They were to build up a big fire as he had something to burn. Then, going to a chest, he took out a small box from within which came a rustling. He said to the two women, 'My mother held a power and that power comes to me but I'll not have it.' He then thrust the box into the flames.

At once a terrible screaming arose from the box, like a human voice in agony, which went on and on until the box and its contents had been reduced to ashes. Then in the dreadful silence which followed, the man said very quietly, 'The power has been destroyed. At last I'm free.'

This grim folk tale reveals the old-time belief that the power of a witch was passed down to her descendants by means of animal familiars, which were handed on at death, but it also indicates how that entail might be broken – by fire.

The 1871 census of Hadleigh shows William, a widower aged 60, lived with his daughter and son-in-law, Joseph and Eliza Wiltshire, at 1 New Road, Hadleigh, although he died in the same year.

H ALSTEAD

Agnes Steadman, spinster, was brought before the assizes at Chelmsford on 28 August 1572, indicted for three crimes of animal damage, bewitchment, and physical torment.

She was alleged to have bewitched three cows worth £4 that belonged to John Rome on 1 May, causing them to languish for three days before dying, and to have bewitched a cow worth 30s that belonged to Owen Norman on 7 June, causing it to become violently ill, and for bewitching Sibyl, wife of Thomas Bentall, yeoman of Halstead, on 1 July, so that she became violently ill for twelve days and feared for her life. Steadman was found guilty on all counts, and was remanded in jail for one year.

Joan, wife of Christopher Fysher, labourer, was tried on the suspicion of bewitching Joan Lewes on 23 September 1595, who languished until 14 October, following which she died. Joan was found guilty and sentenced to be hanged.

H ARWICH

Twenty-seven women from Harwich were found guilty of witchcraft and hanged. The hangings were always a very public affair, drawing large crowds, and the events were advertised on flyers which attracted entertainers and vendors of food. The punishments were meted out from a mansion house called The Three Cups (the site was at 64 Church Street, and is now in residential use), which was owned by Anthony Seward, and used to hold the sessions of the peace. As was the case in other areas, most of the women accused of witchcraft were widows or spinsters.

Elizabeth Hudson and Elizabeth Hanby were accused of witchcraft and went before the justices at Harwich on 20 April 1601, where they were judged guilty and subsequently hanged. Hanby was the eldest of three generations of women who were thought to be descended from witches and to have given birth to witches. Hanby's daughter, Jane Prentice, was tried at the Essex Assizes on 1 August 1634 for bewitching Cecily, the wife of William Field, whereby she died on 20 October. She was acquitted, but faced trial again in 1638, this time with her granddaughter, Susan Prentice.

Elizabeth Hankinson and Alice Babb were also hanged after their trial for witchcraft on 25 August 1601, and on 29 October, Mary Hart was accused of bewitching 7lb of meat which turned putrid. She was found not guilty, but the accusation hung over her, and, fuelled by an apparent dislike by the people of the town, she was found guilty on another charge and hanged a year later.

Margaret Buller, of Dovercourt, appeared with her sister Anne on 4 August 1615, indicted for sending one of Anne Buller's familiars, a bird, to bewitch John, the 13-year-old son of William Camper, yeoman. Camper testified that his son 'fell ill with stomach pains and awoke during the night much frightened and scared with a thing fluttering on his face in his sleep like a bird and he said, pray God Mother Buller did not send me something unto me this night.' Two days later, John was dead. Both sisters were pronounced guilty and hanged.

The trial of Jane Wiggins took place in 1634, where Thomasine, the wife of Richard Hedge, testified that Wiggins told her that she had gone to beg some fish from Anthony Payne, the master of a ship at Harwich (which was being readied for a voyage to sea). He denied her, and she told him not to return in haste. The ship and its crew of sixteen persons were subsequently 'cast away'.

Wiggins also went to the house of one John Hatch for 'fyer,' which was empty but for a girl of about 12 years of age, who refused her because there wasn't enough in the hearth to spare, whereupon Wiggins told the child that she would 'fidle her for it, and immediately after the child was taken strangely sicke and hath continued languishinge and distracted ever since.'

Hedge continued giving her testimony by saying that she was at the house of the said Jane Wiggins, who presently went out:

… after her running to fetch fyer, and was no sooner gon out of her house but thear came from under her bed three things much like Ratts only a little lesse with great staring eyes, and after a wyle gazine (on her) they went away but what they weare (she) knoweth not, nor did the same Jane tell her although she asked her.

Further to that, Hedge went on to say that about the time of the previous Michaelmas, she saw Wiggins carrying two 'imps lyke Ratts but somewhat bigger' in a box, and left one of them at the house of Edward Maiers, who died four days later, and that she sent another of her 'familiars to terrify Margaret Garrettt with pains and lameness because she the said Margaret would give her no starch.'

Jane Wiggins seemed to have been somewhat handy with her 'imps', as she sent 'two Black Birds aboute the bignes of two penny chikins' to strike Mr Seaman's mare.

Clearly Wiggins was not the most popular person among the inhabitants of Harwich at that time, and she was taken before the assizes held at Chelmsford on 26 February 1634 for jail delivery. She was subsequently hanged as a witch for her perceived crimes.

Hatfield Peverel

Over a twenty-five-year period, Hatfield Peverel harboured fifteen suspected witches, and another thirty people were directly involved as husbands or victims of witches. From the series of recorded confessions for the assizes of 1566 and 1579, one can get an understanding of the fear and tension that was caused to the villagers by half-animal, half-demon creatures, all of which were fully credible to them and also to the presiding magistrates, who included the Queen's attorney, Sir John Fortescue (later Chancellor of the Exchequer), and Thomas Cole, Archdeacon of Essex.

An example of the more extraordinary (but by no means exceptional) beliefs circulating the village was a girl who was questioned by Sir John Fortescue. She answered that while she was churning butter, 'there came to her a thynge like a black dogge with a face like an ape, a short taile, a cheine and sylver whystle (to her thinking) about his neck, and a peyre of hornes on his head, and brought in his mouth the key of the milkehouse doore.'

The animal demanded some butter from the milkhouse and then departed. When the girl told her aunt of this encounter, she sent for the priest, who 'bad her to praye to God, and cal on the name of Jesus'. This caused only a momentary diversion, for the familiar reappeared several times.

Sir John Fortescue then turned to Agnes 'Mother' Waterhouse, the suspected witch, and asked her, 'can you make it come before us nowe, if ye can we will dispatche you out of prison by and by', but she replied that she could not call him. Sir John then asked Waterhouse 'when dyd thye cat suck of thy bloud?' 'Never,' she replied. The jailer lifted up the kercher on her head, exposing spots on her face and one on her nose, and Sir John asked her, 'When dydde he sucke of thy bloud laste?' She replied, 'By my faith, my lord, not this fortnyght'.

She confessed that she received the cat from Elizabeth Francis, who willed her to call him 'Sathan', and told her that if she cared for him, he would do for her what she would have him to do.

To test this, she willed him to kill a hog of her own which he did, and she gave him a chicken for his reward, but he first required a drop of her blood. From then, she had to give him blood whenever he did anything for her. She would prick her hand or face, and smear her finger with her blood and then put it to his mouth, which he sucked, then he would lie down in his pot again, where she kept him. However, the marks and spots that would have been made where she said she had pricked her skin were not to be found.

On another occasion, she said that she had felt so offended by one 'Father' Kersey, that she sent Sathan to kill three of his hogs, which he did. Upon his return he told her what he had done, and she rewarded him as before, with a chicken and a drop of her blood, which he ate up clean as he did all the rest, and she could find remaining neither bones nor feathers.

She also confessed that after falling out with one Widow Gooday, she willed Sathan to drown her cow, which he did, and she again rewarded him with a drop of her blood. She also killed three geese belonging to another neighbour in the same manner.

She further confessed to her attempt to send Sathan to hurt and damage the goods of her neighbour, a tailor named Wardol. However, this was unsuccessful because he was so strong in faith. She was also questioned about her church habits. Agnes Waterhouse said that she prayed often, but always in Latin because Sathan forbade her from praying in English.

Her fate was sealed by the evidence given by her neighbours that she had bewitched William Gynee, who had languished and finally died.

Agnes was hanged two days later on 29 July 1566, and it was only at this time that she repented and earnestly confessed that she:

...had been a witch and used such execrable sorcery the space of twenty-five years, and had done many abominable deed, the which she repeated earnestly and unfeignedly, and desired almighty God forgiveness in that she had abused his most holy name by her devilish practices, and trusted to be saved by his most unspeakable mercy.

Elizabeth, the wife of Christopher Francis, yeoman, was accused, along with Agnes Waterhouse and her daughter, Joan, of bewitching an infant child of William Auger, who 'became decrepit'. Before the Attorney General Sir Gilbert Gerard at the assizes at Chelmsford, it was claimed that Francis had learned witchcraft since the age of 12 from her grandmother, 'Mother' Eve. She renounced God and fed her blood to a familiar she was given, the cat called Sathan, who had promised her a rich husband and had killed a man who refused her advances. It was said that Elizabeth commanded the cat to get her another husband, and a child by this man was aborted by witchcraft: Sathan 'bade her to take a certain herb and drink it, which she did, and destroyed the child forthwith. She was alleged to have handed the cat over to Mother Waterhouse in exchange for a cake, instructing her how to manage the animal.

Joan Waterhouse was 18 years of age when she was charged with bewitching Agnes Brown, a 12-year-old girl who became decrepit in her right leg and arm. Joan and her mother had two imps, one in the shape of a toad, and the other of a dog, and it was the latter that she sent to harm Brown. However, after conflicting evidence, Joan was found not guilty, but the trial was the beginning of an unhappy time for people who were disliked by their neighbours, and the cat Sathan made many more appearances in various guises until the last official English execution for witchcraft in 1685 at Exeter.

KELVEDON

Joan Cocke, spinster, of Kelvedon, appeared at the assizes held at Brentwood on 13 March 1567, indicted for the charge that on 1 December 1566, she bewitched Agnes Cryspe, a 1-year-old child, so that from that day she became lame, enfeebled and maimed, and the jurors said her life was despaired of. Cocke was found not guilty, but was also tried for clapping her hands on Richard Sherman's knees, making him lame saying, 'that she defied one Blackbornes wyfe whome the saide Richard Sherman said and reported to be gladde of hir deliveraunce.'

Cocke's daughter was also suspected of being a witch according to a noble's wife, because she could not get butter, and that cows belonging to Belfild's wife's (a woman from Linford, Stanford-le-Hope) had been bewitched so that one had died and two others would produce milk of all colours.

KIRBY-LE-SOKEN

Mary, wife of John Coppin, husbandman, was taken before the assizes at Chelmsford on 17 July 1645, indicted for bewitching Alice, the daughter of William Astin, bricklayer, on 20 July, whereby she died instantly. After witness testimony of Ellen Mayers, Elizabeth Hunt and William Astin, Coppin was found guilty, and sentenced to be hanged as a witch, although she was reprieved after the judgement. She was known still to have been in jail on 11 August 1647.

LAMBOURNE

Alice 'Mother' Nokes, wife of Tom Nokes, of Lamberd Ende (now Lambourne) allegedly became offended when a servant of Thomas Spycer refused to answer a question she put to him; shortly thereafter, one of the horses he was ploughing with fell down with a swollen head and died. Thinking that the servant had beaten the horse about its head, Spycer demanded to know what had happened, to which the servant recounted the story. Spycer went to Nokes and threatened to have her answer for the death of the horse.

Mother Nokes allegedly bewitched the limbs of two servants in the service of Thomas Spycer. One of the servants had snatched a pair of gloves from the pocket of Mother Nokes's daughter, to which Nokes said, 'I will bounce him well enough,' causing his limbs to give out. The other servant was afflicted when the first servant passed the gloves to him to return on his behalf. Mother Nokes afflicted the boy's limbs so badly that Thomas Spycer had to have him brought home in a wheelbarrow, and he was unable to move from his bed for eight days.

On another occasion, Mother Nokes allegedly caught her husband, Mr Nokes, having an affair with the wife of a Lamberd Ende tailor. In revenge, Mother Nokes was said to have told the tailor's wife that she would not keep her nursing child. Shortly thereafter, the child died.

Mother Nokes, when asked to reconcile with Mr Nokes and the tailor's wife, allegedly answered angrily that she 'cared for none of them all as longe as Tom helde on her side'.

Mother Nokes was tried for murder by witchcraft at Chelmsford in April 1579. She was found guilty and 'allegedly' hanged thereafter.

L ANGHAM

Mary Sterling, the wife of John Sterling, yeoman, appeared on 19 December 1642, along with her husband, made 'to answer the inhabitants of Langham.' Sterling had only a short reprieve before she appeared again, this time as a witch who allegedly 'did entereine, employ and feede' two evil spirits, both in the form of moles. It is likely with one of these that she is believed to have bewitched Robert Potter junior to death. Following the witness testimonies of Francis Mills, Isaac Bemish and Grace Norman, Sterling was found guilty on both charges, and sentenced to be hanged at Chelmsford. However, she was 'reprieved after judgement and to remain to gaol until the next gaol delivery.' Sterling appeared in the rolls of the assizes held at Chelmsford on 22 March 1648 on a felony charge.

L AWFORD

Joan Thacher, spinster, was brought before the assizes at Chelmsford on 2 March 1584, indicted for bewitching a horse worth 30s, a cow worth 4 marks, and a pig worth 3s 4d belonging to Nicholas Frends, at Bromley, so that they died. She was found guilty. She was also found guilty on a second indictment that on 29 April she bewitched three cows, ten sheep, and a pig that belonged to John Dixe, so that they died. Thacher was found guilty on a third indictment that on 1 June she bewitched to death a bullock worth 40s, and a cow worth 40s that belonged to Christopher Hansteede.

Rebecca West described to one John Edes at Lawford how she first gave her heart to the Devil as a child, some seven years earlier, while living in Rivenhall.

He had appeared before her and her mother, Anne West, in various guises, but when he appeared as a 'proper young man' who asked Rebecca to turn from God, the Devil that day became her deity, providing for her and protecting her. To Rebecca he was like a father, master, brother and, in due course, would be her lover.

The patriarchal values of one of the chief inhabitants of Rivenhall, George Francis, were to cast a long shadow over the disreputable widow and her daughter, but when his only son was 'cut down', he believed that he had fallen victim to a witch. Rebecca remembered hearing her mother say that 'if Master Francis thought the boy bewitched, surely he was right.'

[Anne West had been described as 'the old Beldam Weste', a reputed witch who was tried for witchcraft in 1641 and in 1642. Although acquitted on both charges, she was popularly believed to be a witch, and was at the centre of the Mathew Hopkins/John Stearne witch-hunts of 1645.]

Although West had condemned herself, Hopkins was looking for even more. Elizabeth Clarke of Manningtree had already given him some information. Having been examined for Devil's marks, such as warts or moles, she then, under torture, broke down and named several other women, including Anne West and her daughter Rebecca. But Hopkins and Stearne needed to know more about an alleged rendezvous with Satan that was mentioned by Anne Leech. Satisfied with the promise of her freedom from Hopkins, West described the story of the sabbat, and of her initiation into the cult of witches. However, it differed somewhat from her earlier statement of events to John Edes, to the effect that the happenings of seven years earlier actually took place in early 1644:

One afternoon, Rebecca was at work when her mother encouraged her to be finished by sunset. When she asked her mother why, she said that she had an appointment in Manningtree and wanted Rebecca to accompany her, but Rebecca was made to promise that whatever she saw at their destination she would keep the closest of secrets.

Her tasks were finished with half an hour of daylight left, so Rebecca and her mother started out on their walk along the road to Manningtree. They arrived at a house, where they met Elizabeth Clarke, Anne Leech, Elizabeth Gooding and Helen Clarke. When asked if her daughter was prepared, Anne West replied that she was, and so, with the women sitting on chairs that had been arranged in a circle, the proceedings began.

Demons shaped like dogs and kittens appeared, jumping into the laps of everyone except Rebecca. When asked whether she wanted to join the witches' society, Rebecca said yes, whereupon she was made to swear on a book that she would keep their secret, even if 'the rope were about her necke, and shee ready to be hanged', and told that if she betrayed them, 'shee should endure more torments on earth than could be in hell'. When Rebecca had given her word, a demon leapt up, kissed her and 'promised to doe for her what shee could desire'.

One evening in the autumn, when Rebecca was going to bed, the demon appeared as an irresistible young suitor. He kissed her on the mouth with lips as cold as clay, and they became married there and then, which was something John Stearne remarked upon later as 'a fearful thing to declare.' Hopkins's own account of the wedding vows state that 'He tooke her by the hand and lead her about the chamber, and promised to be her loving husband till death, and to avenge her of her enemies.' Her heart melted 'and shee promised him to be his obedient wife till death, and to deny God and Jesus Christ.'

Following that, Rebecca confessed that the Devil became her instrument of revenge upon Thomas and Prudence Hart, with whom she and her mother appear to have been bitter enemies. It was Rebecca who was held accountable for Prudence Hart suffering a sudden miscarriage, and later finding herself lamed by a mysterious 'thing'. Hart's son John was also alleged to have been killed by West as an act of vengeance against her husband, Thomas.

Following her story, Rebecca was returned to prison, and Hopkins rode back to Manningtree. The next day (Friday, 18 April), Hopkins relayed the girl's confession to magistrates Sir Harbottle Grimston and Sir Thomas Bowes, and it was recorded by the clerk as evidence. Once signed and sealed, it was ordered that Rebecca West be brought to Manningtree. On Monday, she appeared before the said magistrates, where she recounted her story for a third time, and it was slightly different again. The seven years had shrunk to a month, which meant that her initiation took place just before Elizabeth Clarke's arrest. The confession also specified *maleficia* against named individuals.

Every one of them made several propositions to their familiars. First of all, Elizabeth Clarke desired of her spirit that Richard Edwards 'might be met withall about the middle bridge, as hee should come riding from Eastberghoult in Suffolk, that his horse might be scared, and he thrown down, and never rise again.'

Elizabeth Gooding wished harm upon Robert Taylor's horse, Anne Leech asked for a cow to be lamed, and her daughter Helen wanted a neighbour's pig to die. This left Anne and Rebecca West. The mother asked 'that shee might be freed from all her enemies, and have no trouble', the daughter that her imp might paralyse Prudence Hart down one side of her body. Rebecca West told the magistrates that the witches agreed to meet again, and so went their separate ways.

In the days that followed, more witnesses came forward. One of them, Richard Edwards, confirmed that as he was returning from East Bergholt one evening, and was near Manningtree's middle bridge, his horse had indeed reared up. He said that as he struggled to regain control of the reins, he heard a sound 'much like the shrieke of a polecat.' He was lucky to have avoided a fall, but when he arrived home he was still in a state of shock, and told his wife and neighbours what had happened.

Thomas Hart stated on oath on 23 April 1645 that about eight weeks previously, he and his wife were at the parish church, half a mile from their home, and 'being about twenty weeks gone with childe, and to her thinking, very well and healthfull, upon the sudden shee was taken with great pains, and miscarried before shee could be got home.'

Prudence Hart also stated that 'about two moneths since, being in her bed, in the night, something fell down upon her right side, but being dark, she cannot tell in what shape it was: And that presently shee was taken lame on that side, with extraordinary pains and burning, but recovered again within a few dayes after.' Thomas believed that Rebecca and Anne West were the cause of her pains, 'for that the said Rebecca hath in part of her Confession expressed, that shee had much maliced this Informant, because the said Rebecca West ever thought this Informant to be her greatest enemy.'

Thirty-four women were on remand at Colchester by the summer of 1645, of whom four died (probably from plague) before the assizes. The remaining thirty suspects, including Rebecca West, were moved to Chelmsford for trial on 17 July.

Owing to the wartime disruption of the administration of justice, the judge was not a professional but a Puritan soldier, the Earl of Warwick. There had never been a witch-trial like this before in English history. At the time, Hopkins and Stearne had left Essex to search for witches in Suffolk, but returned as witnesses against several of the accused. Already, it seems, they were courting controversy, having been involved in a tense stand-off in Colchester. Some townsmen had objected to the witch-hunt, possibly because they feared an overfull jail – a threat to order, public health and the public purse.

Rebecca West appeared at the assizes on the witness testimony of John Cutler and Thomas Hart, that on 1 June she 'did enterteine, employ and feede' three evil spirits, one in the likeness 'of a grey catt' called Germany, the second like 'a white katt' called 'Newes', and the third like 'a young man' called her 'husband', with the intention of getting their help in witchcraft and sorcery.

The big revelation, beyond her testifying against numerous other women (including Anne Leech, Elizabeth Gooding, Helen Clark, Anne West, and Elizabeth Clark), was that the 'devel can take any shape, and speake plaine English.' West had seemingly struck a deal with Hopkins and/or the state; she testified against her mother on the charge that she had bewitched John Cutler junior to death, and also against Elizabeth Gooding on charges of having bewitched John Edwards to death. Despite being indicted as a witch herself, Rebecca was not prosecuted for witchcraft.

Nehemiah Wallington, an English Puritan artesan (wood turner) and chronicler, kept extensive journals documenting the battles and skirmishes of the English Civil War period and also wrote about how a supposed coven of witches was found in the Essex village of Manningtree. Of Rebecca West's confession he noted that, 'When she (Rebecca) looked upon the ground she saw herself encompassed in flames of fire, and as soon as she was separated from her mother, the tortures and the flames began to cease. As soon as her confession was fully ended she found her conscience so satisfied and disburdened of all tortures she thought herself the happiest creature in the world.'

In the end, four women were sentenced to be hanged at Manningtree and the remaining fifteen at Chelmsford where, one by one, they climbed the ladder to be turned off by the hangman before a tumultuous crowd. The nine reprieved women remained in jail and would stay there without hope of release until their pardon application was sent to Parliament, a procedure that would take nearly five months. At least one woman died while waiting.

L ittle Baddow

Alice Swallow, spinster, and a common witch, was brought before the assizes at Chelmsford on 2 March 1570, where she was found guilty on the indictment that on 1 April 1569, she bewitched Alice, wife of William Basticke, so that she languished until 1 May, when she died.

L ittle Leighs

Mary Holt, widow, was indicted at the assizes held at Chelmsford on 2 March 1618 for bewitching Margaret Ellis on 25 April, whereby she died on 1 May. She pleaded not guilty, but after the witness testimony of William Ellis was found guilty and held on remand until she was hanged.

L ittle Oakey

Annis Herd, the mother of Annis Dowsing and at least one son, was ill thought of for witchcraft and being a harlot by several residents of Little Oakley, and information was given against her on 17 March 1582 by

John Wade, Thomas Cartwright, Richard Harrison and several other parishioners before Brian Darcey Esquire, one of Her Majesty's justices.

John Wade had twenty sheep and lambs bewitched by Herd so they became lame and died, and five more people also spoke out against her. Two of Thomas Cartwright's cows died after he had annoyed Herd by moving a makeshift road repair; Bennet Lane (wife of William Lane) lost the ability to spin after demanding a dish back from Herd and also lost the ability to make cream after demanding two pence back.

Andrew West, having rescinded on a deal to give Herd a pig, found one of his went mad. Having accused Herd of having an 'unhappie tongue', West's wife suddenly could not brew. Edmond Osborne and his wife also lost the ability to brew after calling in a loan from Herd, which she owed for 'a pecke of Aples'.

While Richard Harrison was in London, his wife accused Herd of stealing ducklings from their nest underneath a cherry tree, and having gone to Herd to 'rate and chide' her, Mrs Harrison soon became very ill, and was convinced that Herd had bewitched her. 'A True and Just Record of the Information, Examination and Confession of all the Witches Taken at St Osyth in the County of Essex' records that within two months, she implored her husband:

> I pray you as euer there was loue betweene us, as I hope there hath been for I haue us pretie children by you I thanke God, seeke som remedie for me against yonder wicked beast (meaning the said Annis Herd), and if you will not I will complaine to my father, and I thinke he wil see som remedie for me, for (said she) if I haue no remedie, she will vtterly consume me.

Herd was not charged for Harrison's bewitchment, nor did she even acknowledge it in her confession, although she did acknowledge the other charges against her. Despite the myriad of witnesses who testified against her, and her inclusion among the 'witches' in the assize record of 29 March 1582, she was indicted for only one charge, that of the great damage done against John Wade in his loss of livestock, for which Herd was sent to prison.

Little Sampford

Joan Preston and Frances Preston, spinsters, were indicted in 1587 for bewitching two cows worth £4 that belonged to George Wynterfludd, so that they died, and were both found guilty. Joan Preston was also found guilty on the further indictments of bewitching two pigs worth 20s that belonged to Thomas Maskall on 31 May, and of bewitching Margaret Haukyn on 20 August. She was subsequently remanded for a year.

Little Totham

At assizes at Chelmsford on 14 March 1610, Anne Pennyfather was indicted for bewitching Robert Thoroke on 23 July 1609 so that his body was wasted and mutilated. Evidence was given by four witnesses: Robert Barnard, William Purr, Robert Hunter and John Austen, but the jury found Pennyfather not guilty.

She could not have been a popular person in Little Totham because William Purr, Robert Hunter, John Austen and five further witnesses – Nicholas Clarke, Annis Garling, Thomas Hawkins, Robert Brocas and Robert Thorrocke – gave evidence that on 6 November she bewitched Mary Clarke with the intention of destroying her. Again, Pennyfather was found not guilty.

Little Wakering

William Skelton, a labourer and common enchanter, and his wife, Margery, appeared before the assizes held at Chelmsford on 2 March 1573, on an indictment for bewitching Dorothy, daughter of John Fuller, yeoman, on 10 July 1571, so that she languished until 30 November, when she died. They were also indicted for bewitching John Churcheman, 'sayler', of Barling, on 16 November, so that he instantly died. They were further indicted that on 29 July 1571 at Barling, they bewitched Agnes Collen, the one-and-a-half-year-old daugher of William Collen, so that she languished for a long time. They were both found guilty of all charges.

Loughton

Joan Mose, spinster, was brought before the assizes held at Chelmsford on 19 February 1590, indicted for the charge that on 28 January, she murdered Richard, the son of Thomas Stace, by 'withcrafte and sorcerie'. She was found guilty and sentenced to be hanged as a witch.

MALDON

At an inquisition taken at the general sessions of the peace held in the Mote Hall in Maldon on 6 July 1573, Alice Chaundler appeared before William Vernon and Thomas Eve, bailiffs, and Edward Coker and Andrew Michaelson, justices of the peace, accused of bewitching 8-year-old Mary Cowper and her father, Francis Cowper, a fletcher (arrow-maker), to death on 3 July. Chaundler had appeared two years previously with the same accusation, but this time, she was further indicted for bewitching to death Robert Briscoe, aged 30 years, his son aged 2 years, and daughter aged 5 years, to death. Chaundler was found guilty and executed for murder by witchcraft in 1574.

After his wife Alice's execution, John Chaundler went to Ellen Smith, his stepdaughter, to demand some money that Alice had given her, but Smith refused, which allegedly caused a falling-out between them. Chaundler was said thereafter to have been unable to keep down his meat after eating, causing him to waste away until his death.

Smith was also alleged to have had a falling-out with the daughter of 'Widow' Webbe of Maldon. On the day it happened, Ellen Smith struck Widow Webbe's daughter, Susan Webbe, on the face, causing the girl to sicken and die two days later. Susan Webbe is said to have cried, 'Away with the witch, away with the witch,' as she languished on her sickbed.

Ellen Smith's son was allegedly turned away by John Eastwood when begging for alms, and went home to tell his mother. Shortly thereafter, Eastwood was taken with a great pain in his body. That night, Eastwood and a visiting neighbour saw a rat run up the chimney and a toad fall back out. They seized the toad in tongs and thrust it into the fire, which caused the fire to burn bright blue and almost go out. This act was said to have caused Smith great pain, to the point where she came to the house to investigate, pretending merely to be enquiring after the well-being of the inhabitants, and Eastwood sent her away with the insistence that all was well.

In her son's confession, Ellen Smith was alleged to have kept three familiar spirits: 'Greate Dicke', contained in a wicker bottle, 'Little Dicke', contained in a leather bottle, and 'Willet', contained in a wool pack. When Smith's house was searched, the containers were found, but the spirits were gone. Ellen Smith is alleged to have been hanged as a witch in April 1579.

The green in South Street, Manningtree, where Hopkins is said to have carried out some of his infamous witch tests. (Darren Hayman)

Manningtree

The 22 acres of Manningtree, wedged between its larger neighbours of Mistley and Lawford, made it the smallest parish in Essex, and it was also the home of Mathew Hopkins, the Witch-finder General. It is said that he carried out some of his business at the White Hart, and that people were hanged on the green in South Street, as well as being drowned from the 'Hopping' bridge along The Walls.

Anne Harvey, spinster, was indicted at the assizes held at Brentwood on 8 August 1594 for bewitching Parnel Woolnett, whereby she died on 16 March. Harvey was also indicted for bewitching two others: Elizabeth Bowle on 26 September 1593, who died on 8 March, and John Bowle on 25 December 1592, who died on 7 October following. Harvey was found guilty on all charges.

Harvey claimed she had been made a witch by Marion Hocket, who, in around 1638–39, had given her three reddish familiars: two small ones like mice, and one slightly larger. Hocket had promised her that 'if shee would receive them, shee should never want so long as she lived.' Since receiving them, she and Hocket had a falling-out, and Harvey claimed to have wanted to return these familiars, 'Littleman', 'Prettyman' and 'Daynty', back to Harvey, but was unable to. They tormented her, causing her to be pained, and 'much torn and troubled in her privy parts', as if these malicious imps 'had pulled her in pieces'. Harvey was indicted, tried and found guilty on charges of having entertained, employed, and fed 'three evil spirits in the form of a red mousse.' She was reprieved after judgement but remanded in jail.

In April 1645, Elizabeth Gooding was accused of causing the death of a horse about nine weeks previously after she was denied cheese that she was looking to purchase. Mary, the wife of John Tayler, shopkeeper, refused to give Gooding (whom she described as a 'lewd woman') half a pound of cheese on credit, which resulted in Gooding sending an imp to 'vex and torment' her. She left the shop muttering words under her breath, and on the same night, one of Tayler's horses fell ill and died. The opinion held by four farriers was that the horse 'did violently beat himself to death', and Gooding was blamed for it. John Tayler also said that he heard Elizabeth Clarke and Anne Leech had accused Gooding of witchcraft in their confessions. It did not help Gooding in promoting her innocence.

This case seems to have been the beginning of a connection between the investigations that were being made into many of the women in the community who were suspected of, or had already confessed to, witchcraft, as well as those with a history of the crime in their family.

Elizabeth Clarke confessed on 25 April that she sent a spirit in the shape of a red dog to kill a Mr Long (by throwing him off his horse to break his neck). The spirit, however, did not perform the task. When asked by the enquiry the reason for this, Clarke explained that 'the power of God was above the power of the Devil.'

Elizabeth Clarke and Margaret Moone were accused of bewitching John, the infant son of Mr Richard Edwards, making him have 'very strange fire, extending the limbs, and rowling the eyes' from which he died, but the blame was also attached to Anne Leech (of Mistley) and Elizabeth Gooding.

Anne Leech also allegedly bewitched two of Richard Edwards's cows. She accomplished this simply by walking by Edwards's pasture. A black cow fell down as she passed, and a white cow died one day after its fellow on the same spot. Edwards had an autopsy performed on the cows, with the result that 'no disease was discovered, which might occasion their death.'

In March 1644, The Manningtree witches were allegedly searched for witches' marks, and marks were allegedly found on all of them, whereupon they were all hanged: Elizabeth Clarke, Elizabeth Gooding and Anne Leech at Chelmsford, and Helen Clark, Anne West, Anne Cooper and Marian Hocket at Manningtree.

Helen Clarke, the daughter of Anne Leech, and housekeeper of Elizabeth Clarke, confessed to keeping a familiar spirit named 'Elimanzer', which she fed with milk-pottage. Elimanzer demanded that Clarke deny Christ, promising her that if she did, she should never want for anything. Helen agreed, and was accused of being in a kabal of witches which included Anne West, Rebecca West, Elizabeth Clarke, Anne Leech and Elizabeth Gooding, who fraternised, read from the Devil's book and corrupted Rebecca West. Grace Glascock, the wife of Richard Glascock, testified on oath before the justices on 11 April that there was some falling-out between Mary, the wife of Edward Parsley, and Helen Clarke, the wife of Thomas Clarke, and that Helen bewitched Mary, their daughter, simply by passing by the Parsleys' door. She was heard to mutter, 'that Mary should rue for all,' whereupon Mary fell sick very suddenly and died within six weeks. Clarke denied this charge, but was nevertheless alleged to have been hanged as a witch for having committed this and one other murder.

Sarah Bright was indicted at the assizes held at Chelmsford on 17 July 1645 that on 25 June she bewitched Anne, the daughter of Henry Woolvett, mason, whereby she died two days later. Bright was found guilty after the testimony of a female witness with the surname Winterglood, the mother of Anne Woolvett, a witness named Applegate and Elizabeth Potter.

M istley

Anne Leach, widow, was hanged at Chelmsford after being found guilty on the evidence given by Mathew Hopkins, John Richard Edwards and Susan Edwards at the assizes on 17 July 1645, of bewitching John, the infant son of Richard Edwards, gentleman, whereby he died on 5 July following. The crime was alleged to have been co-committed with Anne West and Margaret Moone of Manningtree.

O ld Saling

At the assizes held at Chelmsford on 18 July, 1602, Audrey Pond, wife of Robert Pond, was found guilty of 'bewitching to death' a sorrel mare worth £10 that belonged to John Sorrel. She was also found guilty, after the witness testimonies of Emma Cutt, William Elsinge, Richard Weden, Walter Pratt, John Emson and George Bisshopp, of bewitching Thomas Cutt on 6 December, who languished until 3 January, when he died. Pond was subsequently hanged.

RAMSEY

Elizabeth Harvey allegedly claimed that Marion Hockett made her into a witch in around 1638 by making her have a witch's mark. Hockett allegedly brought her 'three things were of a reddish colour', which in pulling and sucking at her, 'made her have the said marks or bigges.' These familiars, which Harvey claimed she tried to send back, allegedly 'tormented her in her bed, in the places aforesaid, as if they had pulled her in pieces.'

Harvey was searched as a witch by Bridget Reynolds, who, on 3 May 1645, gave evidence under oath before the justices at Ramsey, that she had found three such 'Bigges, and about the said scantling.' Marian Hockett had always denied any involvement with witchcraft, but according to her sister, Sara Barton, who was imprisoned at Harwich on suspicion of being a witch, claimed that Hockett had sliced off her witch's marks to avoid detection. Hockett was subsequently executed as a witch.

Following an argument that took place in 1640, during which Francis Stock enraged William Hatting by referring to his wife as a 'scolder', a mysterious snake appeared on a shelf in Mrs Stock's house. When Mrs Stock endeavoured to kill it with a spade, it suddenly vanished as she struck at it, and was nowhere to be found. She was suddenly 'taken sick with extraordinary fits, pains, and burnings all over her body.' Within a week, in death-throes, she cried out that 'Sarah (Hatting) was the cause of her death', and died.

Francis Stock's daughter died within two or three days of the death of his wife and he suspected that Sarah Hatting was culpable for his child's suffering and death.

Francis Stock's second child also became sick and died; it appeared to have the same disease that claimed its sister and mother.

A verbal altercation between Francis Stock's servant and John Hatting, the son of William and Sarah Hatting, turned into a physical one. The very next day, he was taken sick and so continued in a pining and languishing condition, crying out often that Sarah had bewitched him and was the cause of his death, which soon after ensued.

Hatting was searched in 1645 by Bridget Reynolds, the witch-searcher, who claimed that Hatting had 'foure Teats, or Bigges in those parts, almost an inch long, and as bigge as this Informants little finger.'

S† OSYTH

SFourteen women from St Osyth went on trial charged with witch-craft before the local magistrate, Bryan D'Arcy, at Chelmsford on 29 March 1582. Of these, ten were found guilty of 'bewitching to death', which carried the death penalty.

Ursula Kempe was an impoverished woman who made her living as a nursemaid and midwife, and had a reputation as a 'cunning woman' for removing spells from those who believed they were the victims of witchcraft. As an old 'Mother', Kempe was sought by inexperienced young mothers to help with nursemaiding. This was a very risky business: infant mortality was exceptionally high, post-natal care was unknown, and village 'Mothers' were responding to a dire need.

It was Kempe's misfortune that after helping Davy, the son of Grace Thurlowe, by curing an illness he had, her services were refused to act as a nursemaid for Thurlowe's baby daughter. When the girl fell out of her cot and broke her neck, Kempe was suspected of witchcraft. However, ignoring the rumours, Thurlowe consulted Kempe for treatment of her arthritis, for which Kempe suggested a method she had learned from an old wise woman, and would charge 1s. Thurlowe refused to pay the charge, upon which her condition worsened. At this point, she decided to make a complaint to the authorities.

When brought to trial, D'Arcy persuaded Kempe's 8-year-old illegitimate son, Thomas Rabbet, to testify about his mother's activities as a witch. Following this, he offered Kempe leniency if she confessed her guilt, which she did, and con-firmed her son's account. She testified that she had four familiars: two cats called 'Titty' and 'Jack', a toad called 'Pigin', and a lamb called 'Tyffin', and she claimed to feed them on white bread or cake, and drops of her own blood. She confessed that the black cat called 'Jack' had caused the death of Kempe's sister-in-law, while the lamb was used to cause the death of the Thurlowe baby.

Kempe then went on to name other women she claimed were also witches: Alice Hunt, Alice Newman, Elizabeth Bennet and Margery Sammon, who were subsequently brought to court, where they not only confessed to being witches, but also gave the names of further witches: Joan Pechey, Agnes Glascock, Cicely Celles, Joan Turner, Elizabeth Ewstace, Anis Herd, Alice Manfield, Margaret Grevell and Alice Hunt's sister, Anne Swallow.

Kempe was also indicted with Alice Newman for bewitching Edna, the wife of John Starron, whereby she died on 6 October, and for bewitching Elizabeth, the daughter of Richard Letherdall, on 12 February, whereby she died a fortnight later. They were both found guilty.

Alice Newman was also found guilty and remanded in Colchester prison for bewitching several people, including Grace Thurlowe, John Stratton's wife (to her death), Mr Johnson (a tax/alms collector) and his wife (to death), Lord Darcey (whereby he died), and her own husband, William Newman. She had not confessed to any such crime and was accused of being obstinate.

Elizabeth Bennet was a local woman and the wife of a dairy farmer. She was named by Ursula Kempe as having two familiars: one black dog called 'Suckin' and the other 'redde like a Lyon', called 'Lyerd'. Kempe said that she sent 'Suckin' to plague one Willingall to death, as well as the wife of William Willes (who lingered for years), and that she sent 'Lyerd' to plague Fortune's wife and his child, and to Bonnet's wife 'to plague her' in the knee.

Mr Bonnet confirmed that his wife and Bennet 'were lovers and familiar friendes, and did accompany much together'. However, they had a falling-out between them, and later, after speaking with and kissing Bennet, his wife's 'upper Lippe swelled and was very bigge, and her eyes much sunked into her head, and shee hath lien sithence in a very strange case.'

Bennet's own confession came from behind a veil of tears. She said that she had been neighbours with William Byet and his wife and had lived peacefully for a year or so when they began to argue, 'Byet calling her oftentimes olde trot and olde witche, and did banne and curse her and her Cattell', to which Bennet said 'winde it up Byet, for it wil light upon your selfe.' Following this altercation, Bennet admitted that two of Byet's cattle died, and a third dropped to the ground where he began to beat it to death – which was common practice in Byet's home: his wife beat Bennet's swine 'seuerall times with greate Gybets, and did at an other time thrust a pitchforke through the side of one of them.'

Bennet explained her malefic compact happened two years before, in 1580, and took place as she went through the many long steps needed to make bread. The familiar 'Suckin' grabbed her by the coat as she was coming from the mill and would not release her for over two hours until she 'prayed deuoutly to Almightie God to deliuer her from it: at which time the spirite did depart from her.' He followed her home, where he held her fast again, and again she again prayed and was released. Within hours, 'Suckin' appeared again, once by the well, where she was presumably collecting water and once as she was shifting her 'meale' and was again exorcised.

The following day, as Bennet kneaded her bread, 'Suckin' returned with the spirit 'Lyerd'; they grew bold, and scolded her for being 'so snappish', but were again exorcised. They returned again as she made the fire and were again made to depart. They returned again as she stoked the fire and, growing increasingly bold, grabbed her leg, but were exorcised. 'Lyerd' and 'Suckin' came one final time as Bennet was stoking the fire in her oven. They seized her by the hips and said 'seeing thou wilt not be ruled, thou shalt haue a cause, and would haue thrust this examinat into ye burning Ouen.' Bennet struggled and used the fire fork as a wedge to keep her out of the oven, or to beat off the spirits, but she suffered burns up and down her arms.

They came to her two more times while she was in a barn, once while milking, and again she would exorcise them. It was not until Bennet fell out with William Byet, however, that the spirits acted against others. She claimed that 'shee caused Lyerd in ye likenes of a Lion to goe and to plague the saide Byets beastes vnto death,' but that the spirit called 'Suckin' reported to her that he had, of his own accord, 'plagued Byets wife to the death.' She did, however, send 'Suckin' 'to goe and plague the sayde Willyam Byette, to which the sayd spyrite did' because Byet had 'abused her, in calling her olde trot, old whore, and other lewde speaches.'

Bennett supposed that 'Suckin' and 'Lyerd', which she fed with milk and housed in an earthen pot lined with wool, were sent to her by Joan Turner after Bennet 'had denyed the sayde Mother Turner of mylke.' Bennet was held, indicted and tried for the malefic murder of Mrs Byet and 'acknowledged' the felony. She was condemned to be hanged in 1582.

Margery Sammon was given two familiar spirits in the shape of toads from her mother, 'Mother' Barnes, who was described as a notorious witch, who told her to feed and care for them, or to pass them on to 'Mother' Pechey if she would not. Mother Barnes was accused of conspiring with her daughter Alice Hunt to bewitch Rebbecca Durrant after her father, Henry, refused to give them some pork. Durrant died on 24 November, and although Hunt was indicted for her malefic murder, she was found not guilty. However, Mother Barnes never made it to court; she died on 12 February 1582.

Joan Pechey was over 60 years old and the mother of Phillip Barrenger. She had been allegedly described by 'Mother' Barnes, via her daughter Margery Sammon, as 'skilfull and cunning in witcherie', and a woman who could both do 'as much as the said "Mother" Barnes', or 'any other in this towne of St Osees.'

She was alleged to have bewitched Johnson, the tax collector and distributer of alms, after he gave her 'bread was to hard baked for her'. Being an old woman, she presumably should have received a softer loaf and the harder bread should have been given to 'a gyrle or another, and not to her.' She denied any involvement in witchcraft and denied that Mother Barnes had any connection either. She also denied the accusations of incest between herself and her 23-year-old son, Phillip Barrenger, who confessed that 'manye times and of late hee hath layne in naked bed with his owne mother, being willed and commaunded so to doe of her.' Although she was 'committed to prison for suspicion of felony and upon inquisition', she was released by proclamation.

Agnes Glascock was found guilty of having bewitched Martha Stevens, Charity Page and the Pages' child (or ward) to death. Glascock was searched by Annis Letherdall and Margaret Sympson, and despite finding that she had witch's marks on her left shoulder and thigh that looked like they had been sucked, just like Ursula Kempe, she was reprieved. Similarly, Cysley Sellis was alleged to have bewitched John, the son of Thomas Death, to death. Upon being searched as a witch, she was found to bear similar witch's marks, but was found guilty, and remanded.

Joan Turner was accused by Elizabeth Bennet of facilitating witchcraft by sending her the sprits 'Suckin' and 'Lyerd' after she denied her milk. According to Alice Manfield, her own four spirits, 'Robin', 'Jack', 'William' and 'Puppet' (alias 'Mamet'), abandoned her to hide out with 'Mother' Turner (or Ursula Kempe, Margery Sammon or Alice Hunt). She had previously been indicted at Brentwood on 13 March 1581 for bewitching Anne Feast, 'so that her life was despaired of'; George Sparrow; and a pregnant Ellen Sparrow to death, and was found guilty on all charges. She was subsequently remanded for a year at Colchester Castle prison.

Elizabeth Ewstace was accused of bewitching Robert Sannuet so that 'his mouth was drawne awrye, well neere uppe to the upper parte of his cheeke'

The Cage, St Osyth. (Ian Press)

after he 'used threatning speeches' on her daughter Margaret, who was working as his servant at the time (in around 1567). This was not the only crime she was accused of committing against Sannuet, however. She also went after his family and his livelihood. She allegedly bewitched his wife, so that she developed a 'most straunge sicknes, and was deliuered of childe, which within short time after dyed' – a crime which found its origins in the bewitchment of his brother, Thomas Crosse, Felice Oakely's late husband. Crosse originally blamed his illness on Margaret Ewstace, and after Sannuet swore he'd be avenged on her if it was true, Elizabeth allegedly bewitched Sannuet's wife and his livestock. Crosse, who before (in around 1579) was 'verye sickly, and at tymes was without any remembrance' soon 'pyned', and 'coulde neyther see, heare, nor speake, and his face all to bee scratched' and 'woulde alwayes crye out upon the sayde Elizabeth even unto his dying day.' She was accused of having three imps (or spirits), of white, grey and black, which she denied, and she also denied being in any co-conspiracy with Ales Newman.

Felice Okey testified that Elizabeth Ewstace threatened her husband, leaving him for a short while with scratches on his face, and no ability to see, hear or speak, for causing hurt to her geese.

Alice Manfield, who around twelve years previously had shared her two male and two female familiars (in the shape of black cats) with Margaret Grevell, served as a witness against 'Mother' Ewstace, claiming that she had a white, a grey and a black feline familiar which she used to kill a child. Manfield also testified against Grevell, claiming that she had plagued her mother to death.

Manfield was also alleged to have sent her familiar 'Robin' to lame a bull that belonged to Robert Cheston about four years previously, and 'Jack' to lame Cheston himself two years previously, which resulted in his subsequent death. She also claimed to have sent her familiar 'Puppet' to Joan Cheston after she was refused her curds, and after her yard was ruined by the cart of John Sayer, Puppet was sent to ensure that the cart became stuck and would not move. John Sayer confirmed that his cart became stuck when the man thatching his barn refused to thatch Manfield's oven until he got permission to do so.

Around Michaelmas time, all four of Manfield's familiars allegedly took a trip together to assist Cecily Sellis in the burning of Ross's barn and cattle. Her familiar William allegedly gave notice to Manfield for the whole group, claiming that since she would soon be apprehended, they would go to work for Ursula Kempe, Margery Sammon, Ales Hunt or Mother Torner (aka Joan Turner). Mansfield was indicted as a witch, but not charged as one. She was, however, charged with arson. She was found guilty of co-conspiring with Cecily Sellis to burn Richard Ross's barn and a 'field of grain worth 100 marks.'

Margaret Grevell was alleged by Alice Manfield to share these four feline familiars with her for seven years, and according to Manfield she caused her imps to 'destroy seuerall brewinges of beere' that belonged to Reade and Carter (Carter likewise testified against Grevell on this charge) and also a number of batches of bread. Nicholas Stickland accused Grevell of preventing his wife's butter from churning and causing the untimely demise of a calf, and although Grevell was accused (again by Manfield) of the murder of Elizabeth Ewstace's husband, she was indicted for the malefic murder of Robert Cheston. She was searched as a witch, but the witch-searchers said that 'they cannot judge her to haue any sucked spots upon her body.' She was found not guilty of causing Cheston's death, and was acquitted.

At the end of the trial, only Ursula Kempe and Elizabeth Bennet were sentenced to hang.

In 1921, two female skeletons were unwittingly discovered by a Mr Brooker, a tenant in St Osyth carrying out some work in his garden in the village. Both bodies had been bound with chains and pinned down with iron rivets driven through their knees and elbows, which was a common method of stopping witches rising from the grave and causing further trouble in the village. One skeleton was badly damaged, but they were believed to be Ursula Kempe and Elizabeth Bennet. It was not unusual for women accused of witchcraft to be hanged in their village and then buried in local unconsecrated ground. Mr Brooker, having some knowledge of the history of witches in the village, cashed in on the discovery by arranging visits from local people wanting to

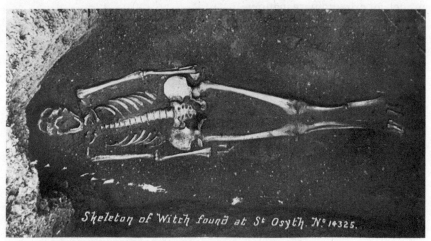

The skeleton of Ursula Kempe, found in 1921.

see the witches' skeletons. It was only when the house burned down in an unexplained fire in 1932 that interest waned in what was now believed to be the body of Ursula Kempe, and the remains were reburied at the site.

An Examination of Witches in 1645

At the examination of Rose Hallybread, taken before the justices on 6 May 1645, she claimed that about eight years previously, Susan Cook, Margaret Landish and Joyce Boanes (all of whom stood suspected of witchcraft), each brought an imp to her house, and then together with one of her own imps, Joyce Boanes carried them to the house of Robert Turner to torment his servant for refusing to give them a few chips. Hallybread said that the servant became ill forthwith, and often barked like a dog, and that 'shee believeth that the said four Imps were the cause of his barking and sicknesse.'

Joyce, the wife of William Boanes, confessed before the justices that she carried one of her imps, called 'Rug', to the house of Rose Hallybread, and then collected three more imps from Susan Cook and Margaret Landish to take them to the house of Robert Turner to kill his servant, whereupon he 'hath oftentimes crowed like a Cock, backed like a Dogge sung tunes, and groaned.' Boanes said that her imp 'made the said servant to barke like a Dog; the Imp of the said Rose Hallybread inforced him to sing sundry tunes in his great extremity of paines; the Imp of the said Susin Cook, compelled him to crow like a Cock; and the Imp of Margaret Landish made him groan in such an extraordinary manner.'

Susan Cook confessed that she took her imp, called Besse, together with one imp each from Rose Hallybread, Joyce Boanes and Margaret Lindish, to the house of one John Spall to kill ten or twelve sheep, because she, 'being with childe, desired to have some curds of the said Spall's wife, which she refused, either to give or sell to her.' Cook further confessed that about a week previously, she, together with Joyce Boanes, Rose Hallybread and Margaret Landish, sent four imps to the house of one Robert Tender to torment his servant, for he had refused to give her a sack full of chips. She also said that she, accompanied only by Landish, sent imps to the house of Thomas Mannock, where they killed six or seven pigs, and gave the reason that the wife of Mr Mannock refused to give to her 'such reliefe as shee desired, telling this Examinant, that shee was a young woman, and able to worke for her living.'

Rebecca Jones, widow, and a former servant to a John Bishop of Great Clacton, was brought before the assizes on 9 May 1645, indicted for having committed two murders by witchcraft. She confessed under oath that some time around 1620, a handsome young man, a person she later came to believe was the Devil, had come to her door, pricked her wrist and carried a drop of blood away on his fingertip. Around three months later, she was travelling to St Osyth to sell her master's butter when she met a man with great eyes, who wore a ragged suit, and she was 'much afraid of him'. He gave her 'three things like to Moules having foure feete apiece, but without tayles, and of a blacke colour,' named 'Margaret', 'Amie' and 'Susan'. The man instructed her to nurse them 'untill he did desire them againe', to feed them milk, and to use them for acts of vengeance and murder. Jones went on to say that 'the first time shee imployed any of the said things, shee sent one of them to kill a Sowe of one Benjamin Howes of Little-Clacton in the County aforesaid; and the said Sowe was killed by the said Impe accordingly.'

Jones also confessed that she sent 'Margaret', one of her imps, to kill Thomas Bumstead, whereby he died about three weeks later, and because he had beaten Jones's son for eating some honey he had found in their house, Joyce Boanes sent the imp Amie to kill Bumstead's wife, who died a short time after. Her third imp, 'Susan', she sent 'to afflict the childe of one Mistris Darcy of St Osyth, but did withall bid the said Impe it should not hurt the said child too much, and come away againe.' Jones was found guilty of both murders and was hanged.

Margaret Landish, also known as 'Pegg the Witch', was also alleged to have sent her imp to John Spall's home, 'where the said imp killed ten or twelve (of his) sheep.' She also sent her imp to kill 'six or seven hogges' belonging to Thomas Mannock. Both Spall and Mannock were apparently being punished for their lack of charity.

Landish confessed to having a familiar, but claimed she entered into a malefic against her will only 'eight or nine weekes' previously. It was done to her when she was 'lying sicke by the fire side in her owne house, something came up to her body, and sucked on her privie parts, and much pained and tormented her.' The thing which tormented her was an imp sent by Susan Cook. Landish denied all other charges.

Sible Hedingham

Katherine Harrys and Agnes Smythe (alias Lawsell), both of whom were spinsters, were indicted at the assizes held at Braintree on 15 July 1588, that on 20 August they bewitched George Glascock so that he died.

They both pleaded not guilty, but the jurors returned a guilty verdict and they were sentenced.

At the assizes held at Chelmsford on 5 July 1589, Joan Prentice, a spinster who lived in the Almshouse of Sible Hedingham, pleaded not guilty to the charge that on 10 February, she bewitched 2-year-old Sara Glascock, who languished and then died on 28 February.

Prentice confessed that she became a witch in about 1583, after the Devil appeared unto her at her almshouse at about 10 p.m., 'being in the shape and proportion of a dunnish colored ferret, having fiery eyes.' She said that she was alone in her chamber, sitting upon a low stool and preparing herself for bed when the ferret, standing with his hind legs upon the ground and his forelegs settled upon her lap, looked into her eyes and said, 'Joan Prentice, give me thy soul. I am Satan; fear me not, my coming unto thee is to do thee no hurt but to obtain thy soul, which I must and will have before I depart from thee.'

Prentice said that he demanded 'that of her which is none of hers to give, saying that her soul appertained only until Jesus Christ by whose precious blood-shedding it was brought and purchased', to which the ferret said, 'I must then have some of thy blood', which she granted, offering him the forefinger of her left hand. The ferret took it into his mouth and, 'setting his former feet upon that hand, sucked blood thereout, insomuch that her finger did smart exceedingly.' When she asked for the ferret's name, it answered 'Bid'; and then presently vanished out of her sight suddenly.

The ferret returned about a month later at the same time of night as she prepared to go to bed. She said that she was sitting upon a little stool when it leapt upon her lap:

> ...and from thence up to her bosom, and laying his former feet upon her left shoulder, sucked blood out of her left cheek, and then he said unto her, 'Joan, if thou wilt have me do anything for thee, I am and will be always ready at thy commandment.' And thereupon she, being a little before fallen out with the wife of William Adams, willed the ferret to spoil her drink which was then in brewing, which he did accordingly.

During the course of her examination, Prentice also accused Elizabeth, the wife of Michael Whale, and Elizabeth, the wife of John Mott, the town cobbler, of being 'well-acquainted' with 'Bid', but did not go so far as suggesting they had killed or harmed anyone with him. The women were brought to the assize on the weight of this claim, but were freed on insufficient proof.

Prentice further confessed that the last time the ferret appeared to her was about seven weeks past, at which time she was going to bed, and 'he leaped upon her left shoulder and sucked blood out of her left cheek and, that done, he demanded of her what she had for him to do?' She sent 'Bid' to Glascock's house to 'nippe one of his children a little, named Sara, but hurt it not,' because she was refused alms at the Glascock home. 'Bid' allegedly returned the following night, and claimed he had given the Glascock child a nip which would soon kill her. Prentice and 'Bid' soon fell out; she called him a villain and he disappeared, never to return. The jury found Prentice guilty of the malefic murder of Sara Glascock, and she was conveyed to prison, where around two hours later she was hanged in Chelmsford.

Elizabeth Esterford appeared before the assizes on three occasions in 1593, each time to answer the accusation of bewitchment. In March, she was indicted with bewitching a sorrel mare and a sorrel bald horse and a cow, belonging to Henry Spencer, making them sick. She escaped a prison sentence, and in July went before the justices again, this time accused of bewitching Anne Bidford on 1 December, whereby she died on 28 December. Esterford pleaded not guilty and the jury found in her favour. However, the third indictment was for bewitching a mare, a horse and two cows worth £10, belonging to Henry Spencer, and on this occasion she was found guilty. Her sentence was not recorded, but at the assizes held at Chelmsford on 18 March 1594 she was remanded for one year for practising witchcraft.

Sible Heddingham was where the last recorded case of 'swimming' in England occurred. In 1863, an 80-year-old man by the name of 'Dummy' lived alone with his three dogs in a hut on the outskirts of the village. He was thought by many to be French, but was quite mute. One night, when he was drinking in a public house called The Swan, he was accused of casting the 'evil eye' over a woman called Emma Smith, who subsequently became ill. When Dummy declined to go home with Smith to lift the spell, she became hysterical and attacked him with a stick. He was dragged down to a nearby stream by a mob, who had decided to test him as a witch by swimming. He was thrown off the bridge, and every time he tried to climb up the bank he was pushed back. Two local women rescued him and took the soaking-wet old man home, but he never recovered, and died several days later in the local workhouse. Emma Smith and a young man called Samuel Stammers were both accused of murder as they had used the evidence of a 10-year-old girl to cause the poor man's death, and were sentenced to six months hard labour for his death.

S tebbing

Margaret Hogden, a spinster of Stebbing, alleged to be a common witch and enchantress, appeared before a group of jurors at the Easter sessions at Chelmsford on 25 February 1582, for bewitching and enchanting Margaret, wife of John Hull, at Stebbing, so that she languished until 21 January and then died the following day. The jurors returned a verdict that Hogden feloniously, and of her malice aforethought, murdered the said Margaret Hull.

Two further indictments were brought against Hogden at the assizes held at Witham on 29 July 1583. She was alleged to have bewitched Mary, the daughter of John Hayward, husbandman, whereby she languished until 30 July. Hogden was found not guilty, and pardoned. She was also accused of bewitching Elizabeth Robinson, who died on 11 June following, but the jurors again reached a verdict of not guilty. Hogden was hanged as a witch later in 1583.

S tisted

On 31 March 1589, Joan Cunny, spinster, appeared before Anthony Mildemay, Esq., at the assizes held at Chelmsford, on several indictments, which included bewitching Barnard Gryfeyn on 3 February, whereby he languished; of bewitching Elizabeth, wife of Henry Fynch, whereby she died on 17 February; and of bewitching Joan Danishe on 20 April, whereby she was afflicted in her right leg. Cunny was found guilty on these charges and others that involved her use of familiars, named 'Jack' and 'Jill', to hurt many people over a span of sixteen to twenty years.

Joan Cunny confessed to sending her familiars to hurt John Sparrow's wife, and to knock over a stack of logs in John Glascock's yard, and also to hurt William Unglee, a Miller of Stisted, but they were unsuccessful. Instead, the familiars hurt Barnaby Griffen, one of Unglee's workers.

When she was refused a drink by Harry Finch's wife because she was too busy, Cunny also confessed that she had sent her familiars to seek revenge upon her. Finch's wife had great pain in her head and in the side of her body for a week, after which she died. These claims against Cunny were also supported with evidence given by her children and grandchildren.

Cunny confessed that she learned the art of witchcraft from 'Mother' Humfrey. Humfrey allegedly showed her how to pray to the Devil by kneeling and making a circle on the ground. Joan Cunny was hanged immediately after the trial.

Cunny's daughter Margaret, a spinster, was indicted at the assizes held at Chelmsford on 5 July 1589 that on 28 February she bewitched John Gwian, whereby he lost the sight of one eye. Cunny pleaded not guilty, but was found to be guilty, and was sentenced to one year imprisonment and six pillory sessions.

Margaret Cunny was also indicted with her sister, Avice Cunny, spinster, that by 'witchcraftes, enchauntementes, charmes, and sorceries', on 10 March, they bewitched Jeremy Browne, who became gravely ill in his left leg. They were both found guilty. Avice Cunny was further indicted with bewitching Richard, the son of William Franck, on 1 August, whereby he died. She was found guilty and sentenced to be hanged, but pleaded pregnancy, which was concurred by a jury of matrons.

STOCK

On 20 September 1574, Agnes Sawen, a spinster, of Stock (latterly of Little Waltham), was brought before the quarter sessions at Chelmsford, indicted for witchcraft. She was accused of practising her art on her neighbour, Christopher Veele, son of Roger Veele, 'so that the feet of the aforesaid Veele were and still remain curved, and one of his feet is wasting within so that he can scarcely use them to his very great hurt'. It appears that Agnes was eventually pilloried and confined in Colchester jail for one year, despite her protestations of innocence.

THAXTED

Elizabeth Taylor, wife of John Taylor, a labourer in Thaxted, was indicted for the charge that on 10 April 1573 she bewitched Alice Holmes, the daughter of William Holmes, a basket-maker of London, who languished until 14 April, and then died. Elizabeth pleaded not guilty, but was judged guilty and sentenced to death.

She was also accused of bewitching Agnes Townsend, daughter of William Townsend, a carpenter of Thaxted, on 10 October 1573, who languished for ten days until she died. She was judged guilty despite her 'not guilty' plea.

Alice Hynckson, widow, of Thaxted, was sentenced to one year's imprisonment and four sessions on the pillory, despite pleading not guilty to bewitching four cows, valued at £4, and seven ewes, valued at 20s, the goods of Thaxted husbandman James Jarvys, on 20 January 1572, all of which died within four days. Hynckson later died of plague while on remand in jail on 4 May 1575.

Agnes Dix, wife of labourer John Dix, of Walter Belchamp, was indicted that on 1 May 1574 she bewitched Richard Hayward, who languished for fourteen days, and also for bewitching Elizabeth Potter, wife of John Potter of the same place, who languished until she died on 30 January following. She was found not guilty on both charges.

✝ Heydon Garnon

At the assizes held at Chelmsford on 3 July 1589, the jurors heard that Joan Dering, spinster of Theydon Garnon (in the district of Epping Forest), bewitched Alice Odell on 20 December, whereby she languished until the enquiry. Odell pleaded not guilty, and was found so.

Dering was also found not guilty on a further indictment that on 30 November 1588, she, by 'witchcraftes, enchautementes, charmes, and corceries,' bewitched pails of milk belonging to Stephen Clerke, so that his servants, try as they might, were unable to use it to make cheese.
Dering was brought before the assizes again on 24 July 1589, indicted with bewitching James, the son of John Bennet, who still languished. She was found not guilty.

✝ Horpe-le-Soken

Francis Miller gave information under oath before the justices on 29 April 1645 that she was employed by the neighbours of Margaret Moone to search her, and found three long 'teates', or 'bigges', in her 'secret parts', which seemed to have been recently sucked. Moone's two daughters were also searched, and were also found to have 'bigges in their privy parts'. Judith Moone testified that she had fought with her mother about two weeks before her apprehension: Margaret wanted her to go and collect wood, but Judith didn't feel like doing it. The next night, she felt something crawl into bed with her, and although she searched, she could not find anything. The testimony of four more witnesses: Mary Philips, Elizabeth Harris, Susan Burles and Philip Tumnor, were taken under oath before the justices, and they all concurred with Miller's information.

One day after her father had done some labour for Moone, Joan Cornwall became sick. She suffered from strange fits and shrieking out, and so continued to languish for a month, and then died. Margaret Moone was blamed for her death, but only confessed to bewitching to death some cattle from the stocks of Henry Robinson and Stephen Cookers, and for bewitching Philip Daniel's horse so that it fell and broke its neck while pulling Daniel's wagon down a hill. She was sentenced to be hanged as a witch, but died prior to her execution.

Margaret Grevell was a 55-year-old woman from Thorpe, who, according to Alice Mansfield, shared her four feline familiars for seven years. In a statement made to Justice Brian Darcey five days before the case was brought before him at the assizes at Chelmsford on 29 March 1582, Mansfield said that Grevell had 'caused her imps to destroy several brewings of beer', which belonged to Reade and Carter (Carter likewise testified against Grevell on this charge), and a number of batches of bread.

Grevell had also been indicted on the confession of Mansfield for the malefic murder on 20 November 1581 of Elizabeth Cheston's husband, Robert. Grevell was subsequently searched as a witch, but the witch-searchers said that, 'they cannot judge her to have any sucked spots upon her body.' She was found not guilty of causing Cheston's death, and acquitted.

Nicholas Stickland, a butcher in Thorpe, testified to Brian Darcey that Margaret Grevell had sent her son to buy a rack of mutton from him, and he asked him to return in the afternoon. A few days after turning Grevell away, Strickland's wife was unable to produce butter. He also blamed Grevell for causing the untimely demise of a calf. Margaret Grevell was remanded at Colchester for her mischievous actions.

TOLLESBURY

Katherine Pullen, a spinster and common witch of Tollesbury, appeared at the assizes at Chelmsford on 2 March 1573, where she pleaded not guilty to the indictment of bewitching Joan, wife of John Dannynge on 12 November 1572, so that she instantly died. Pullen was found guilty and was subsequently hanged.

Upminster

Susan, wife of Henry Barker, was brought before the assizes at Chelmsford on 15 July 1616 on four indictments of witchcraft. On 10 February she was alleged to have bewitched Mary Stevens at Hornchurch, whereby she became consumed and mutilated. Despite evidence given by William Stevens and Anne Stevens, she was found not guilty and acquitted. Anne Stevens also alleged that, on 8 September 1615, Barker 'did take upp a scull out of a grave with the intention of using it for witchcraftes, charmes and sorceries'. Again, Barker was found not guilty and was acquitted.

Her luck ran out, however, after witnesses Francis Ramme, Esquire; Anne Ashen; William Stevens and Thomas Dyeson were called to testify that in Upminster on 7 April Barker bewitched Edward Ashen senior, whereby he languished at Hornchurch until he died on 11 May. Witnesses Katherine Coppin, Agnes Ashen, Mary Dyason and Margaret Asghen also testified against Barker on a second indictment of 'murder by witchcraft', that on 20 February she bewitched Edward Ashen junior, whereby he died three days later. Barker was found guilty of the two crimes and was sentenced to be hanged.

Wakes Colne

Katherine Lawrett, spinster, appeared before the assizes held at Chelmsford on 14 March 1610, indicted with murder by witchcraft. Witnesses John Lawrett, William Lawrett, Henry Allum, William Kinge, Constance Kinge, Annis Tayler and Annis Cooke testified that on 22 August 1609 Lawrett bewitched Susan Kinge, who died seven days later. Lawrett was found guilty and sentenced to be hanged as a witch.

Waltham

At the assizes held at Colchester on 21 July 1564, Elizabeth Lowe, wife of yeoman John Lowe, of Great Waltham, allegedly bewitched John Cannell, Robert Wodley and John Wodley, a 3-month-old infant of Chelmsford. The child languished for two days and then died. Lowe pleaded not guilty, but was found guilty on all three counts, but pleaded her pregnancy.

Lowe is supposedly the first person ever to be indicted by the 'Act agaynst conjuracions Inchantments and Witchcraftes'. Her case was brought forth less than a year after the act was passed by the Elizabethan government. While Lowe's case contained a few unusual details for the time, it was, nevertheless, not very rare. On one occasion, she allegedly bewitched her husband making him lame, which was not unheard of for the period. Elizabeth Lowe's case does provide something that others seem unable to, however. Lowe's case is recorded in detail and, on top of being the first one indicted under the 'Act agaynst conjuracions Inchantments and Witchcraftes', it can be clearly read as an example of how and why witches were persecuted to calm social anxieties.

Richard Dunne, a labourer, and Agnes Dunne, spinster, appeared at the assizes at Chelmsford on 3 July 1589, indicted that on 12 February they bewitched a gelding worth 40s belonging to Thomas Warren. They pleaded not guilty, but the jurors found them guilty as charged. The same Richard and Agnes Dunne were also indicted that on 1 July they bewitched Henry Ladd so that he languished, a charge upon which they were found not guilty. Similarly, an indictment of bewitching one Simon Beck also returned a not guilty verdict.

WALTON-LE-SOKEN

Margery, wife of John Grew, husbandman, was indicted at the assizes at Chelmsford on 17 July 1645 that she bewitched John, son of Samuel Munt, husbandman, so that he died instantly. Grew pleaded not guilty, but after the evidence given at the trial by John Poonant, Samuel Munt, Helen Mayer and Elizabeth Hunt, she was convicted for the crimes of 'murder and raising spirits' (she had a familiar shaped like a jay that may have been used in this crime and hanged as a witch.

WIMBISH

At the assizes held at Chelmsford in April 1579, evidence was presented in several incidents against 'Mother' Margery Staunton, late of Cole End, Wimbish, most of which resulted from the refusal of various individuals to give in to her demands for items such as leather thongs and milk. The first of these occurred when she was turned away from the home of Richard Saunders after she tried to borrow yeast from Mrs Saunders. Staunton was said to have left the home murmuring, and shortly after her departure, the Saunderses' baby became violently sick. When Mr Saunders picked up the infant to comfort it, the cradle continued to rock of its own accord, and would not stop until a visiting gentleman stabbed it repeatedly with his dagger.

Staunton was also alleged to have gone to the home of William Corner and to have demanded various things, including a piece of leather, from Mrs Corner, which was denied her. She then demanded to know how many children she had, to which Mrs Corner replied that she had one. The child soon suffered from sweating and chills, and started shrieking, staring, wringing and writhing until it was thought it would die.

It was further alleged that Staunton went to Robert Cornell's home twice to ask for milk from Mrs Cornell, who turned her away, and barred the door on both occasions due to the suspicion that Staunton was a witch. The second time she came to the house, Staunton drew a circle in the dirt with a knife outside the front door, marking it with the compass points. When asked, she claimed to be digging a 'shitting house' for herself. The next day, Mrs Cornell left the house through that door, and is said to have been taken sick with an illness that caused her stomach to swell up as if she were pregnant until she feared she would burst. Apparently, she was still not in good health by the time of the trial.

Staunton allegedly demanded milk from John Cornell and took offence when she was denied; immediately afterwards, his cattle were said to have given gory stinking blood instead of milk, and one of his cows became so stricken that it never recovered.

Staunton was also alleged to have gone to the home of Robert Lathburie to make demands, but was sent away. Shortly after her departure, twenty of his hogs were said to have fallen sick and died, and one of his cows was afflicted such that it became three times more likely to become lost. Lathburie burned one of the dead hogs in an attempt to save the rest.

The wife of the vicar of Wimbish became a victim of Staunton one day while the vicar was away. After being denied her demands, Staunton was said to have touched the vicar's son, causing him to become sick. When the vicar returned home, the child recovered perfectly within an hour and resumed playing.

Staunton allegedly went to Robert Petie's house and demanded numerous things from his wife, and even accused Mrs Petie of stealing a knife from her. When Staunton was sent away, the Peties' little child became so ill for a week that it nearly died.

Thomas Prat wrote a detailed account of these incidents, accusing Staunton of witchcraft, and had it witnessed by Thou Farrour and Thomas

Swallowe, following which he delivered the document to Master George Nichols. Subsequently, Staunton faced and argued with Prat at his home, during which Prat scratched her face with a needle. In response, she told him he had a flea on him, causing him to be tormented in his limbs the next night. Prat wrote up this incident and submitted it as evidence against Staunton, which further enraged her. She allegedly went by his home carrying grain, which Prat wanted for his chickens, and snatched some of it from her. After they had eaten it, three or four dozen of them were said to have died, with Prat suggesting that they had been bewitched. 'Mother' Staunton was found not guilty.

W ITHAM

Joan Haddon, a spinster and common witch of Witham, was indicted at the assizes at Chelmsford on 4 July 1560 with bewitching Joan Bowltell and Thomas Emmerye, among others, as well as fraudulently taking money from them. She pleaded not guilty on the count of witchcraft, but guilty on other counts, upon which confession she was pardoned after the consideration of the court.

Elizabeth Harris, spinster, was brought before the assizes held at Chelmsford on 4 March 1588, indicted with bewitching Gilder, the son of Thomas Wayland on 18 November 1587, whereby he died eleven days later. She was found not guilty.

W IVENHOE

Alice Dixon, widow, was indicted at the assizes at Chelmsford for bewitching Thomas, the son of John Mumford, husbandman, whereby he died on 20 July. After the testimony given by Margaret Mumford, Dixon was found guilty. While standing accused of witchcraft, Dixon said that she discovered that Mary Johnson was responsible for the suffering and death of Elizabeth Otely's 2-year-old child. This act of murder was administered through familiar magic: Johnson set her imp, a thing in the shape of a rat with no ears, to attack Otely's child, and through contamination, Johnson gave the child an apple and a kiss which made it sicken and die within three days. When Dixon accused Johnson to her face of causing this harm, she allegedly responded, 'that if she did it, she did it, she could but receive punishment for it.' Alice Dixon was hanged at Chelmsford on 17 July 1645.

Mary Johnson, the wife of Nicholas Johnson, a Wivenhoe seaman, was indicted at the assizes at Chelmsford on 17 July 1645, for entertaining and feeding three evil spirits, two in the likeness of rats, and one in the likeness of a mouse, procuring their help in witchcraft. She pleaded not guilty, but after the evidence given by Ellen Mayors, Elizabeth Hunt, Anne Darrell and Priscilla Briggs she was found guilty and sentenced to be hanged as a witch, but was reprieved after judgement.

The same witnesses gave evidence that Johnson also bewitched William, son of George Durrell, fisherman of Wivenhoe, on 20 June, who languished for five days and then died. Johnson was found not guilty.

Johnson was also accused of bewitching the young daughter of Annaball Durrant. She is alleged to have used the word magic, called the child pretty, and spread *maleficium* through touch, by stroking its cheek, thus poisoning it though a kind of bad magic spread through bread and butter. The child cried in agony and fell lame, and continued like that for eight days. Although her mother consulted a local surgeon, he could find no natural cause for her child's ailments, nor administer a natural cure, and the child died.

Durrant allegedly had a vision of Johnson that while she cleared an out-house following the death of her child, she was suddenly 'struck with a lameness in her arms, and they became so rigid that three or four people that came to help were unable to bend her arms, and (she) lost her voice.' She had to be carried home by friends, and she remained in that condition for two weeks before she returned to health. In April 1645, George Durrant, having encouraged his wife, Annaball, to testify against Mary Johnson, suddenly gave a great shriek, and said Johnson 'would be his death, and had a great swelling risen up in his breast, and now lies sweating, and in great extremity.' He continued to cry out, 'It comes; it comes, now Goodwife Johnson's Imp is come. Now she hath my life.' Durrant did not seem to be hallucinating about this torment, and the buzz of a hornet filled the room.

Despite the elaborate nature of these accusations, Johnson is also accused of making Elizabeth Otley herself suffer from extreme pain, with loss of appetite, and insomnia, presumably to weaken her enough physically and psychologically that she would believe Johnson's many claims of innocence. Otley, however, decided she had been 'witched', and then 'un-witched' herself through a long fist fight where she made Johnson's teeth bleed.

Johnson was finally found guilty of malefic murder through bewitching Elizabeth, the daughter of Daniel Occlam, on 20 June, who languished for five days before she died. However, after being sentenced to be hanged as a witch, she was reprieved.

WOODHAM FERRERS

Margaret Mynnet was brought before the assizes held at Chelmsford on 26 July 1593, on three indictments: that on 31 March she bewitched Isabel Lorken, who languished until she died on 2 April, and that on 1 April she bewitched Joan Lorken, with the same outcome on 6 April, and of bewitching Simon Fylpott (Philpott) on 19 April, who died on 26 April. Mynnet pleaded not guilty, but was found guilty and hanged.

Robert Copping appeared at the assizes on 8 August 1664, indicted that on 8 May he bewitched William Slater, who died two days later. Evidence was given at the trial by Margery Slater, John Aylett and one other, whose name was omitted from the records. He was found guilty and hanged.

ELEVEn

Witches and Halloween

Double, double toil and trouble;
Fire burn, and caldron bubble.
Fillet of a fenny snake,
In the caldron boil and bake;
Eye of newt, and toe of frog,
Wool of bat, and tongue of dog,

(Bonnie Blanton)

Adder's fork, and blind-worm's sting,
Lizard's leg, and owlet's wing,
For a charm of powerful trouble,
Like a hell-broth boil and bubble.

Double, double toil and trouble;
Fire burn and cauldron bubble.
Scale of dragon, tooth of wolf,
Witches' mummy, maw and gulf
Of the ravin'd salt-sea shark,
Root of hemlock digg'd the dark,
Liver of blaspheming Jew,
Gall of goat, and slips of yew
Sliver'd in the moon's eclipse,
Nose of Turk and Tartar's lips,
Finger of birth-strangled babe
Ditch-deliver'd by a drab,
Make the gruel thick and slab.
Add thereto a tiger's chaudron,
For the ingredients of our cauldron.

Double, double toil and trouble;
Fire burn and cauldron bubble.
Cool it with a baboon's blood,
Then the charm is firm and good.
O well done! I commend your pains;
And every one shall share the gains;
And now about the cauldron sing,
Live elves and fairies in a ring
Enchanting all that you put in.

By the pricking of my thumbs,
Something wicked this way comes.

(*Macbeth* Act IV, Scene I ('Round about the Cauldron Go'))

The history of Halloween, like any other festival's history, is inspired by traditions that have been handed down through ages from one generation to another, but as the process goes on, very gradually, much of it becomes distorted with newer additions and alterations.

Riding a broomstick while wearing a pointed hat and carrying a black cat, or sailing the seas in sieves (that witches on the continent were alleged to be capable of) are the images of the witch taken from the most iconic and infamous characters from fairytale, folklore and fiction. Given the true story of paranoia and persecution during the witch-hunts that led to the execution of some 50,000 European people believed to have been witches – men as well as women – between 1500 and 1800, these images attract yet frighten us. Some early witches did carry brooms, but not for flying of course: they were used to cleanse an area or room before a healing ritual could be performed in it. In those days, it didn't take much for that to be the start of vicious rumours to be circulated.

Witches have had a long history with Halloween. They would gather twice a year when the seasons changed: on 30 April – the eve of 'May Day' – and on the eve of 31 October, 'All Hallow's Eve' (from the old English 'halwen'). In AD 835, the Roman Catholic Church made 1 November a Church holiday to honour all the saints. Although it was a joyous holiday it was also the eve of All Souls Day, and in medieval times it became customary to hold vigil and pray for the dead. The three days between 31 October and 2 November saw pagan and Christian celebrations intertwined: it was the highest period in Wiccan witchcraft, abounding in superstitious observances, and on these nights, after arriving on broomsticks, the witches would celebrate a party hosted by the Devil. Superstitions told of witches casting spells on unsuspecting people, transforming themselves into different forms and causing other magical mischief. Bonfires were also lit to scare off the supernatural creatures that struck fear into superstitious hearts.

In the days of early England, there were Druids – the priests of the Celtic people, who were often called the 'men of the oaks.' They served as the bards, teachers, healers, judges, scribes, seers, astrologers and spiritual leaders of the ancient Celts. They conducted rites and rituals, divined the future, healed the sick, kept the history of their people and addressed legal matters within their communities. These wise men and women were highly revered and wielded authority second only to the king's.

They were also alleged practitioners of human sacrifice, and worshipped the Sun God and 'Cernnunos', the 'horned hunter of the night'.

To them, Halloween was sacred because their Sun God receded to the underworld on 31 October, which is why darkness increased and light decreased, according to their reckoning. As darkness set in they would put on their white robes and hoods, and carry sickles and Celtic crosses as they began a torchlit procession.

At the beginning of the procession, a male slave was killed and dragged by a rope fastened to his left ankle. The Druids would walk until they came to a house or a village, where they shouted the equivalent of 'trick or treat.' The treat was a slave girl or any female to be given to the Druids. If the people refused a girl as a 'treat', the blood was taken from the dead slave and used to draw a hexagram or six-pointed star on the door or wall of the village. Spirits of the 'horned hunter of the night' were invoked by the Druids to kill someone through fear in that house or village that night.

If the house or village gave a girl as a 'treat', the Druids put a pumpkin with a face carved in it in front of the door or gate of that place. Inside the pumpkin was a candle made of human tallow to keep evil spirits away. Thus, the Jack-O-Lantern was (and is) a sign of cooperation with Satan. Halloween was not harmless.

Halloween was the foremost holiday of the Celtic year, and was also popularly known as 'Samhain' or 'Sah-ween', when, according to the belief of Celts, the ghosts of the dead populace could easily and effortlessly mingle with the living citizens at this particular time of the year. It was believed that it was the time when the souls of the departed moved to the other world, and they were all honoured by the lighting of bonfires. Huge crowds would congregate to sacrifice fruits, vegetables and even animals to aid them on their journey to the different world.

The custom of wearing costumes and masks at Halloween is also of Celtic tradition, attempting to copy the evil spirits or placate them. The practice of dressing up in costumes and going begging door to door for treats dates back to the Middle Ages and includes Christmas wassailing. In Scotland, it was known as 'guising'; masqueraders carrying lanterns made out of scooped-out turnips would visit homes at Halloween to be rewarded with cakes, fruit and money. This trick-or-treating resembles the late medieval practice of souling, when poor folk would go door-to-door on Hallowmas (1 November), receiving food in return for prayers for the dead on All Souls Day (2 November).

The first reference to 'guising' in North America was in 1911, and another reference to ritual begging on Halloween appears (place unknown) in 1915, with a third reference in Chicago in 1920.

The Pilgrim Fathers left Plymouth on the *Mayflower* on 16 September 1620, leaving behind them the intolerance the country held for them. They had been persecuted by the Church and were considered traitors and renegades who defied the authority of King James I. They believed that they were true Christians, and were determined to 'purify' the Christian Church and return to a scripture-based service. They were outspoken in their protest against the British, and resented the Catholic Church of England. After a few years of failed attempts to try to settle in different parts of England, they went to the 'new world' in North America, where they could continue with their own intolerant ways. They took everything they would need to survive in such an isolated place, and also some things they really didn't need. Their belief in witches and their legends spread and mixed with the beliefs of the Native Americans, who also believed in witches.

The Legend of Jack-O'-Lanterns

Jack was an Irishman, reputed to have been a stingy drunkard. Legend states that he tricked the Devil into climbing an apple tree for a juicy apple and then quickly cut the sign of the cross into the tree trunk, thus preventing the Devil from coming down again. After making the Devil swear that he wouldn't come after his soul in any way, it didn't prevent him from dying anyway.

When he arrived at the gates of heaven, he was turned away because he was a mean drunk, and so, desperate for a resting place, he went to the Devil. The Devil, true to his word, turned him away. 'But where can I go?' pleaded Jack. 'Back where you come from,' said the Devil. The night was dark and the way was long, and the Devil tossed him a lighted coal from the fire of Hell. Jack, who was eating a turnip at the time, placed the coal inside and used it to light his way, and since that day, he has travelled the world over with his Jack-O'-Lantern in search of a place to rest.

Irish children carved out turnips and potatoes to light the night on Halloween. When the Irish went to America in great numbers in the 1840s, they found that a pumpkin made an even better lantern, and so the 'American' tradition came to be.

Considered by some to be evil, it has been a customary practice for children in many countries to dress in costumes and travel from house to house in order to ask for treats, with the question 'Trick or Treat?' – the trick being to perform mischief on the homeowners or their homes if no treat is forthcoming.

The earliest known use in print of the term 'trick or treat' appeared in Blackie, Alberta, in 1927. Halloween provided an opportunity for real strenuous fun, and no real damage was done except to the temper of some who had to hunt for wagon wheels, gates, wagons, barrels, etc., much of which decorated the front street. The youthful tormentors were at back door and front demanding edible plunder with the words 'trick or treat', to which the inmates gladly responded and sent the robbers away rejoicing.

Dispelling
†he Myth

More witches have been hanged in the county of Essex than any other in all of England. Most of the convictions were based on precarious evidence. At a time of religious hysteria, prejudice, and fear that a pact had been made with the Devil to do his work, confessions were attained in unreliable circumstances or extracted through torture, and the accusers may have had other motives for seeing the discredit, punishment, or even the death of a rival or a troublemaker from their village.

Incredibly, not one case of anyone brought to trial accused of witchcraft provided empirical proof, and yet up to ninety 'witches' were hanged between the late sixteenth and early seventeenth centuries in Essex alone. However, the irrational dislike and hatred of one unfortunate individual was not restricted to the years of the witches; belligerent group behaviour, group animosities and greed have been, and will always be, a part of our society.

The witches themselves were nothing like the stereotype of the carbuncled hags shrieking incantations around a cauldron full of devilish potions. They were ordinary people who were often the convenient scapegoats for anything from a death in the village to the failure of crops. Individuals would often have been branded a witch after falling out with a neighbour. Their practice of witchcraft was the magic created by the understanding of some members of communities of the healing properties of herbs and their application for various ailments. Whilst they were blamed for a variety of unidentifiable and inexplicable illnesses of animals as well as people, those accused of being witches were rarely associated with the effects of plague, even though this would have ideally served witnesses and accusers at hearings and trials as part of the evidence given against an individual accused of bewitchment. Unlike their European counterparts, English witches were not usually blamed for storms or for sexual impotence.

In the village of Boreham, which lies about 4 miles north-east of Chelmsford, there were 351 deaths recorded between 1560 and 1603, and from these are the examples of the 'strange' fate of two young men in the village who were crushed to death while digging in a sandpit, and another inhabitant who fell into a stream and drowned; there was no suggestion that they were believed to have been bewitched, and the verdicts given were 'death by misfortune'.

There was an emphasis on the strangeness of an event; for example, if a huge tree suddenly fell on a windless day, or if a normally clean woman 'was on a sudden so filled with lice, that they might have been swept off her cloaths with a stick', especially when the lice were 'long, and lean, and not like other lice.' When people blamed witches they did it not out of mere ignorance, but because it explained why a certain misfortune had happened to them, despite all their precautions – why, for example, their butter did not 'come'. There is an account of a woman who could not have success with her butter; she tried feeding the cows on better food, tried scalding her butter pans, and finally, in desperation, used the old counter-witchcraft charm of sticking in a red-hot horseshoe, and the butter came.

The amount of pain involved – either physical or emotional – and the ability of physicians to deal with the phenomenon, were partly relevant. The shortfall in medical knowledge was often masked with accusations of witchcraft if the physicians could find no 'naturall distemperature of the body'. It is perhaps no coincidence that witchcraft beliefs and accusations declined because of an alleged advance in medical techniques during the seventeenth century.

Witches were, above all other things, suspected of killing human beings, and those whose death was ascribed to witches characteristically languished for some time before they died. In fact, out the 214 people who stated at the assizes that a period of illness (often between a month and a year) had lapsed after being allegedly bewitched, only seventeen were said to have died of immediate effect. Animals or children were allegedly bewitched if the enemy of the witch, for example, their owners or parents, led a godly life that the curses of a witch had no effect upon.

Parish registers illustrate the high mortality rate of the period, especially of infants, but these do not peak at the times of supposed deaths by witchcraft. Nor does it seem to have been death at childbirth that was automatically blamed on witches; witchcraft was characteristically a relationship between two fully grown people.

During the witchcraft persecutions, many of the elderly who were brought to trial accused of being witches were murdered or permanently disabled through being made to confess, and those found not guilty who survived would have been mentally scarred. Being found not guilty at their trial did not exclude them from further persecution. The label of a witch remained with them, and, branded as outcasts, they were abandoned by society as surely as if they had carried the plague. No one, family or friend, would be seen associating with them, and invariably they were banished to the edge of the village or town by the townsfolk. Without any shelter, food or saviour, they would waste and die. It is most likely that many were innocent victims who may have suffered from common illnesses now known to come with advanced age, such as cognitive decline and dementia, not to mention the various physical maladies of old age, such as rheumatism, arthritis, epilepsy and stroke (even men and women with cataracts were seen as being possessed by the Devil). The associated behaviours would also often have been misinterpreted as signs of witchcraft and sorcery. This is not to say that there were instances where evil connotations could not be ruled out, but with today's understanding of mental illness, many of the characteristics and the often peculiar behaviours would have been recognised.

Prosecutions and executions for the crime of witchcraft declined and eventually came to an end during the seventeenth and eighteenth centuries, and by the early twentieth century, witchcraft was dead; no more than an old wive's tale used to scare children.

The decline occurred in all European countries where witch-hunts had taken place, and wherever ecclesiastical or temporal authorities had brought witches to trial. It was marked by an increasing reluctance to prosecute witches, the acquittal of many who were tried, the reversal of convictions on appeal, and eventually the repeal of the laws that had authorised the prosecutions.

Sarah Wrench

Sarah Wrench had been wrongly assumed to have been a witch. As an alleged witch, her grave, which is by the north wall of the chancel at St Edmund's church in East Mersea, was covered by the locals with a metal cage (or 'Mortsafe', which was invented around 1816) to keep her from returning from the dead and troubling the neighbourhood. A cast iron plaque on the grave is marked: 'Sarah Wrench died 6th May 1848 aged 15 years and 5 months.'

The grave of Sarah Wrench, 'the Caged Witch' of St Osyth. (Debbie Borrett)

The result of a previous enquiry with the church wardens was that she was not a witch, but that she was a young girl who had a child out of wedlock, and as such was considered a bad influence on the parish. Why she was buried on the north side of the church, and who paid for the cage and the inscription on the grave, is not known, but the fact that she was laid to rest in the unconsecrated part of the cemetery (where felons and suicides were placed) gave rise to rumours that she was a witch.

Her status would have made her body attractive to grave robbers. This was due to the necessity for medical students to learn anatomy by attending dissections of human subjects, which was frustrated by the very limited allowance of dead bodies – for example, the corpses of executed criminals – granted by the government, which controlled the supply.

Helen Duncan

Scotland's last witch, spiritualist Helen Duncan, was found guilty by the jury at the Old Bailey of contravening section four of the Witchcraft Act of 1735 – in 1944. She was arrested in Portsmouth alongside three members of her audience as she conducted a séance, for fear her 'powers' could reveal military secrets during the Second World War. Duncan, a housewife and mother of six from Callander near Stirling, was said to have displayed the 'gift' of medium with the spirit world from an early age, and a prominent feature of her sittings was her ability to emit 'ectoplasm' from her mouth during her trances – a stringy white substance that is supposed to give form to spirits and allow them to communicate.

It was at a séance that Duncan reportedly summoned the spirit of a dead sailor who had lost his life alongside 800 others during the sinking of the Royal Navy warship HMS *Barham*. The ship had been sunk by a German U-Boat in November 1941, but had not been officially declared lost until the following January (the government had chosen to keep it secret in order to mislead the enemy and maintain morale). On 19 January 1944, another séance Duncan was holding in Portsmouth was interrupted by a police raid where she and three members of the audience were arrested and remanded in custody by Portsmouth magistrates.

Duncan was originally charged under section four of the Vagrancy Act of 1824, under which most charges relating to fortune-telling, astrology and spiritualism were prosecuted by magistrates in the twentieth century. This was considered a relatively petty charge and usually resulted in a fine if proved. She was eventually tried by jury at the Old Bailey and found guilty of contravening section four of the Witchcraft Act of 1735 (which carried the heavier potential penalty of a prison sentence), and was imprisoned despite the Prime Minister, Winston Churchill, describing the whole episode as 'obsolete tomfoolery' in a memo to the then Home Secretary, Herbert Morrison.

On her release in 1945, Duncan promised to stop conducting séances, but was arrested again during a séance in 1956. She died at her home in Edinburgh a short time later, on 6 December 1956

The Scottish Parliament rejected a petition to pardon her in 2008, and in England, the Criminal Cases Review Commission wouldn't reopen the case as they said it wasn't in the public interest.

The prejudices created by the Christian Church had created an image of the witch that has been associated with evil, heathenism and unrighteousness. Gerald Brosseau Gardner was an amateur anthropologist and archaeologist who was also an English Wiccan and was known by the craft name 'Scire'. He was instrumental in bringing witchcraft back out of the shadows in the 1950s to show the public that it wasn't dead, it had just been hidden. There is renewed interest in witchcraft, and witches profess to believe and practise it with a sense of pride and confidence. The believers in the New Age movement have understood witchcraft from its true perspective, and spiritualism and the occult are still thriving today: people still want to know what comes after this life.

Glossary

Assizes	These were justices of the Court of King's Bench, justices of the Court of Common Pleas and Barons of the Exchequer of Pleas who travelled around the country on five commissions, upon which their jurisdiction depended. Their civil commissions were the commission of assize and the commission of *Nisi Prius* (the court of original jurisdiction). Their criminal commissions were the commission of the peace, the commission of *Oyer* and *Terminer* (to hear and determine) and the commission of jail delivery.
Familiar (or familiar spirit)	A supernatural being that helps and supports a witch or magician. Traditionally, a familiar is an animal, but some are said to be humanoid. Familiars often have special powers of their own. When witchcraft is portrayed as a type of communication or alliance with evil forces in order to gain magical powers, a familiar may be considered a type of demon.
Folk	Of or originating among the common people.
Lore	A body of traditions and knowledge on a subject or held by a particular group and typically passed from person to person by word of mouth.

Pagan (from the Latin for 'country-dweller') A blanket term typically used to refer to religious traditions which are polytheistic or indigenous. Christianity spread more quickly in major urban areas (like Antioch, Alexandria, Carthage, Corinth, Rome) than in the countryside and soon the word for 'country dweller' became synonymous with someone who was not a Christian, giving rise to the modern meaning of 'pagan'. In the late twentieth century, 'Paganism', or 'Neopaganism', became widely used in reference to adherents of various New Religious Movements, including Wicca.

Rump Parliament The name of the English Parliament after Colonel Pride purged the Long Parliament on 6 December 1648 of those members hostile to the Grandees' intention to try King Charles I for high treason.

CREDITS

Dee Gordon, Reverend Stephen Hulford, Sue Kendrick, George Knowles, Deborah J. Martin, Dr Kirsten C. Uszkalo (head of the Witches in Early Modern England Project and editor of *Preternature*), William Wallworth.
The Hadleigh and Thundersley Community Archive
The Essex Record Office, Chelmsford
All uncredited images can be found on Wikimedia Commons.

BIBLIOGRAPHY

A Complete History of Magick, John Locke, 1715

A Confirmation and Discovery of Witch-craft, John Stearne, 1648

'A True and Just Record of the Information, Examination and Confession of all the Witches Taken at St Osyth in the County of Essex', 1582

A True Relation of the Arraignment of Thirty Witches at Chelmsford in Essex, 1645

A Tudor Anthropologist: George Gifford's Discourse and Dialogue, Alan Macfarlane, 1977

'A Wizard of Yesterday', *The Strand Magazine*, Arthur Morrison, 1900

Chelmsford Chronicle, 20 February 1857, 9 November 1900

Compendium Maleficarum, the witch-hunter's manual, 1608

Daemonologie, King James I, 1597

Encyclopaedia Britannica, 1888

Folklore, Vol. 76, No. 3 (Autumn, 1965)

Leechcraft: Early English Charms, Plant Lore, and Healing, Stephen Pollington, 2000

Melampronoea, or, A discourse of the polity and kingdom of darkness together with a solution of the chiefest objections brought against the being of witches, Henry Hallywell, 1703

Malleus Maleficarum (The Hammer of (the) Witches), Heinrich Kramer, 1486

Newes from Scotland, 1591

Old Kittery and her Families, Everett S. Stackpole, 1903

Our Country Vol 1, Benson J. Lossing, 1877

Select Cases of Conscience Touching Witches and Witchcraft, John Gaule, 1646

The Anglo-Saxon Minor Poems, Elliott Van Kirk Dobbie, 1942

The Apprehension and Confession of Three Notorious Witches (Anon), 1589

The Dark World of Witches, Eric Maple, 1962

The Discovery of Witches, Mathew Hopkins, 1647

The History of Rochford Hundred, Philip Benton, 1867

The Imperial Gazetteer of England and Wales, 1866

'The Witches of Dengie', Autumn 1962 issue of *Folklore*, Volume 73

Trials of the Lancashire Witches, Edgar Peel, 1985

Witchcraft in Early Modern Britain, Prof. James A. Sharpe, 2001

Witchcraft in Tudor and Stuart England, Alan MacFarlane, 1970